P9-CQL-865

THE METROPOLITAN
MUSEUM OF ART NEW YORK

Newsweek / GREAT MUSEUMS OF THE WORLD

NEW YORK, N.Y.

**GREAT MUSEUMS
OF THE WORLD**

Editorial Director—Carlo Ludovico Ragghianti

American Editor—Henry A. La Farge

THE
METROPOLITAN
MUSEUM OF ART NEW YORK

Texts by:

Licia Collobi Ragghianti
and the Curatorial Staff of the
Metropolitan Museum of Art

Design:

Fiorenzo Giorgi

Published by

NEWSWEEK, INC.
& ARNOLDO MONDADORI EDITORE

ISBN 0-88225-241-0

Library of Congress Card No. 77-17667

©1978—Arnoldo Mondadori Editore—CEAM—Milan

©1978—Photographs Copyright by Kodansha Ltd.—Tokyo
All rights reserved. Printed and bound in Italy

INTRODUCTION

A. HYATT MAYOR, *Curator Emeritus of Prints,*
The Metropolitan Museum of Art, New York

The years after the Civil War found factories tooled for unprecedented production, new fortunes, open political corruption, cities exploding in social turmoil, and just a few people eager to better things. It was in this climate that in 1870 the Corcoran Gallery was founded in Washington, the Museum of Fine Arts in Boston, and the Metropolitan Museum of Art in New York under different conditions that produced widely differing careers. In the cultural desert of Washington, the Corcoran stayed still for years. The Museum of Fine Arts, favored by the relative stability of Boston, by inherited money and a tradition of giving, by Harvard's historians and connoisseurs, got private donations for an immediate start. But the Metropolitan had hard going in New York. The new rich were building private galleries in their Fifth Avenue houses, and thought that the city could do quite well with The New-York Historical Society, going since 1804, that already had a matchless library of local history, a sizeable Egyptian collection, many American portraits, and about 250 European paintings—some really fine—given in 1868 by Thomas J. Bryan. But the Society's well-born trustees lacked the breadth of sympathy to embrace the changed times and to venture an enlargement of function.

So after much parley, 27 trustees for a new museum were elected in January 1870. In April the brilliant lawyer, Joseph H. Choate, drew up a far-sighted charter for "encouraging and developing the study of the fine arts and the application of the arts to manufacture, of advancing the general knowledge of kindred subjects, and, to that end, of furnishing popular instruction and recreation."

In the spring of 1871 the Metropolitan and its sister, the American Museum of Natural History, applied for city funds to the reigning political boss, William Marcy Tweed. Boss Tweed at once offered to take over the museums in order to acquire a gloss of respectability for his threatened dictatorship and to profit from the construction of costly buildings. Choate offered a compromise: the city should pay for building and upkeep, while the trustees should keep title to the collections. This dual control binds the Metropolitan to demonstrate its usefulness to the taxpayers when it asks the city for its yearly subsidy. These recurrent petitions make the Museum sensitive to public reactions, explain the effort that it puts into exhibitions and the care with which it presents its collections. As a result, more people go today to the Metropolitan than to local baseball games.

But in the beginning, with not even a building, the founding fathers needed something to show for a start. The first gift came promptly—a Roman sarcophagus offered by J. Abdo Dabbas, the American consul in Tarsus, prophetic of today's great archaeological collections. In 1870 a public subscription secured from Paris 174 European paintings that included a good Poussin. This first purchase was presented to the public in the rented attic of Dodworth's Dancing Academy on Fifth Avenue at 54th Street. The Museum outgrew these quarters in 1874 when it bought a huge collection of antiquities excavated by Luigi Palma di Cesnola on Cyprus, where this Italian soldier of fortune had been made American consul to reward him for fighting on the Union side in the Civil War. Cesnola himself came to help the trustees unpack and install his bulky finds in the Metropolitan's second home in an ample house on 14th Street. Cesnola used the purchase money to dig again on Cyprus for a second collection. When he sold this to the Metropolitan in 1876 he returned to the Museum as its eventual director until 1904. Despite the financial crisis of 1873, which depressed world enterprises for about five years, the Museum's permanent red-brick home was designed by Calvert Vaux for Central Park, which he had also designed. There in 1880 the Trustees themselves, for the last time, unpacked the collection as the carts trundled it slowly uptown to the open fields at 82nd Street.

The move to the new building launched an impetus that has never ceased to gather strength. In 1887 Catherine Lorillard Wolfe bequeathed 143 paintings, many of the Barbizon School, along with the Museum's first purchase fund, which eventually paid for Renoir's *Mme. Charpentier and Children* in 1907 (the first important Renoir ever bought by a museum), Goya's *Bullfight*, Delacroix's *Rape of Rebecca*, and Winslow Homer's *Gulf Stream*. The first great paintings came in 1888 when the Metropolitan's second president, Henry Gurdon Marquand, bought 37 pictures especially for the Museum. With extraordinary perspicacity, he selected the van Dyck and one of the Vermeers illustrated here, as well as three Hals portraits and two by Rembrandt, and works by Petrus Christus, Ruysdael, and Gainsborough. In 1889 Erwin Davis gave the first pair of Manets ever to enter a public collection, the *Boy with a Sword* and *Woman with a Parrot*.

Thirty years of struggle had made a provincial museum with a unique collection of Cypriote sculpture. Then it took to the air under a double impact. In 1901 Jacob S. Rogers died, naming the Metropolitan as his residuary legatee. When the Rogers Fund became available in 1904 it amounted to nearly $5,000,000, the income of which was to be used "for the purchase of rare and desirable art objects, and for the purchase of books for the library of said Museum." The Metropolitan could finally compete with the world's greatest museums. In time the Rogers Fund bought 26—nearly one quarter—of the treasures illustrated here. The second thrust came in 1904 when J. P. Morgan took over as president until his death in 1913.

Morgan's mastery drove the Museum into high gear. In 1905 Sir Caspar Purdon Clarke, director of the Victoria and Albert Museum, became director of the Metropolitan, and Edward Robinson, director of the Museum of Fine Arts in Boston—and the only well-trained American archaeologist— came as assistant director, then full director from 1910 to 1931. Morgan engaged Roger Fry to buy paintings, which he did brilliantly for some five years until the two men quarrelled. Fry, and then his assistant, Bryson Burroughs, who came to help him in 1906 and remained as curator of paintings from 1909 to 1934, bought the paintings by Giotto, Carpaccio, Bosch, Breughel, Ingres and Delacroix illustrated in this book, as well as Tintoretto's *Doge Alvise Mocenigo Presented to the Redeemer*, Rubens' *Wolf and Fox Hunt*, Botticelli's *Three Miracles of St. Zenobius*, and, in 1913, the first Cezanne ever purchased by any museum. Also, in 1913 Benjamin Altman's bequest of Chinese porcelains, Renaissance sculpture and goldsmith's work extended to the great paintings illustrated here—those by Dürer, Botticelli, Hals, Ruysdael, Rembrandt's *Portrait of a Young Man*, Vermeer's *Girl Asleep*, and Velazquez' *Supper at Emmaus*. The Metropolitan could begin to be proud of its paintings from before 1800.

But paintings after 1800 were thinner until 1929 when Mrs. Henry O. Havemeyer and her family gave nearly 2,000 works of art of all kinds for almost every section of the Museum. The spectacular part of the collection were the paintings, often bought with the advice of Mary Cassatt. This book reproduces her paintings by van der Goes, Bronzino, Corot, Manet, Degas, El Greco's *Cardinal* and *View of Toledo*, Goya's *Majas on a Balcony*, Cezanne's *Mont Ste. Victoire*. Her astonishing series of works by the Impressionists at one jump made the Metropolitan indispensable for the study of French nineteenth-century painting. The exhibition of the Havemeyer Collection was doubly cheering in the misery of the early Depression. In spite of the ensuing lean years, the Museum managed to buy a predella panel belonging to the Raphael altarpiece that J. Pierpont Morgan, Jr. had given in 1917, Watteau's *Mezzetin*, van Eyck's *Crucifixion* and *Last Judgment*, and Titian's *Venus and the Lute Player*. In 1944 Jules Bache willed the Museum the Crivelli *Madonna*, Titian's *Venus and Adonis*, Rembrandt's *Standard Bearer*, Velazquez' *Maria Teresa*, Watteau's *French Comedians*, and Goya's little *Manuel Osorio* with cats and birds. In 1937 Harry Payne Bingham gave Rubens' *Venus and Adonis*. In 1943 the Metropolitan subsidized the Museum of Modern Art, getting in return 40 works of modern art that had become "classic," such as two Cézannes, three

Matisses, Picasso's *Woman in White* and *La Coiffure*, to which Gertrude Stein's will in 1946 added her massive portrait by Picasso. In 1951 Samuel A. Lewisohn left the Gauguin, Douanier Rousseau, van Gogh's *L'Arlésienne* all illustrated here, as well as Seurat's sketch for *La Grande Jatte*. Van Gogh's *Self Portrait*, also shown here, together with many paintings of the School of Paris, was willed by Adelaïde Milton De Groot in 1967. Thirteen early Italian paintings, among them Sassetta's *Journey of the Magi* (page 66) were added through the bequest of Maitland Griggs in 1943. In 1969 the extraordinary bequest of Robert Lehman brought the great paintings illustrated on pages 67, 68, 70, 94, 95, 114, 119. While these splendid gifts were coming in the Museum bought Caravaggio's *Musicians* in 1952, Rembrandt's *Aristotle with a Bust of Homer* in 1961, El Greco's *Vision of St. John* in 1956, Georges de La Tour's *Fortune Teller* in 1960, Velazquez' *Olivares on Horseback* in 1952 and his *Juan de Pareja* in 1971. The galleries now fairly represent European painting, emphasizing the Netherlands because New Yorkers are still vaguely aware of their Dutch beginnings, and the Impressionists because Americans liked them so soon.

The paintings department took charge of drawings for the first 90 years. Cornelius Vanderbilt started the collection in 1880 by giving 670 Italian seventeenth- and eighteenth-century drawings. In 1910 Mrs. George Blumenthal gave three by Matisse, the first such drawings to enter any museum. Various curators of paintings bought outstandings drawings, such as ten by Degas from his estate sale in 1917, three Leonardo pen sketches and his black-and-red chalk *Head of the Virgin*, Michelangelo's study for the Libyan Sibyl in 1924, an album of 50 Goyas, brilliant Venetian drawings from the Biron Collection, and Rubens' pen preparations for the woodcuts of the *Garden of Love*. Georgia O'Keeffe gave Fauve and Cubist drawings from the Stieglitz Collection in 1949. The bequest of Walter Baker has brought many fine drawings, and the Robert Lehman Collection contains an extraordinary abundance of work by the greatest masters. The collecting of drawings has become more systematic and active since a special department was formed in 1960 under Jacob Bean. The new department has organized distinguished exbititions, some in collaboration with the Morgan Library.

The Department of Prints, now Prints and Photographs, was founded in 1916 when H. B. Dick bequeathed his extensive collection, rich in Whistlers, along with a purchasing fund. William M. Ivins, Jr., the curator until 1946, bought prints with prophetic perspicacity. The Junius Spencer Morgan Dürers came in 1919. Rembrandt's late etchings in rich impressions were bequeathed by Mrs. Havemeyer and Felix M.M. Warburg and his family in 1941. The Warburg gift included superb early Italian and Northern engravings. The collection now contains fine impressions of practically every great printmaker, one of the few comprehensive series of designs printed for craftsmen, many commercial and ephemeral prints, and many of the great illustrated books printed since 1460. Alfred Stieglitz started the photographic collection by giving some of his work in 1928 and then gave Pictorialist work that he had used in *Camera Work*. With the help of David Hunter McAlpin the Museum has bought much early photography. In general, the print collection is smaller than those in Vienna, Paris and London, but spreads over a wider field than any.

So long as the Museum had only the departments of painting and of Greek and Roman art, everything else fell into the limbo of the decorative arts. One of the first sections to split away was the Department of Medieval Art. The bulk of the medieval collection came in 1917 when J. Pierpont Morgan, Jr. gave 7,000 objects that had been on loan from his father for ten years. The elder Morgan, that collector of collections, had purchased the Hoentschel Collection of medieval woodwork, ivories, Mosan and Limoges enamels on copper as well as the incomparable Zvenigorodskoï collection of Byzantine enamels on gold. Among the other donors were the Pratt family, who gave to almost every department of the Museum. Mrs. Harold Irving Pratt donated the early Franco-Flemish *Annunciation* tapestry, one of the most lyrical of the Museum's medieval wall hangings. 11

The department's later effort went into making The Cloisters. This branch museum originated in 1914 when the sculptor George Grey Barnard set up in New York the stones of cloister ruins that he had gathered in France. Barnard's little museum seemed to John D. Rockefeller, Jr. to offer stay-at-homes their only chance to see the great creation of the Middle Ages—its architecture and architectural sculpture. So in 1925 he bought Barnard's assemblage to move into the park that he was giving to the city on the hill of Fort Tryon. On the highest point of Manhattan Island, over the grandest view of the Hudson, Rockefeller and James J. Rorimer helped to fit these cloisters together with an imaginative simplicity that has stood the test of time. When this branch museum opened in 1938, Rockefeller had already given it the Unicorn Tapestries, the most romantic picture cycle of the waning Middle Ages. He followed this with funds that served to buy the fourteenth-century tapestries of the *Nine Heroes*, the chalice from Antioch, the Virgin from the rood screen of Strasbourg Cathedral, the ivory cross from Bury St. Edmunds, and the celebrated *Annunciation* triptych by Roger Campin. The Cloisters has made an unforgettable setting for medieval music and miracle plays.

The story of the Middle Ages continues in the Department of European Sculpture and Decorative Arts, which started in 1907 when J. P. Morgan gave outright the eighteenth-century French porcelain, furniture and woodwork in the Hoentschel Collection. In 1910 Thomas Fortune Ryan's gift of Rodin sculpture laid the foundation for the remarkable group of French sculpture after 1600 given by the Paul Foundation. Brilliant Sèvres porcelains and furniture decorated with Sèvres plaques were donated by the Kress Foundation in 1958 when R. Thornton Wilson was building up the European ceramics until they now represent every important factory. The Museum's first French royal furniture—made by Riesener for Marie Antoinette—came in 1920 from William K. Vanderbilt, and has been followed recently by the princely pieces with which Mr. and Mrs. Charles Wrightsman have furnished the great rooms that they have installed. In 1974 the Sheafer Collection brought porcelains and some of the finest German eighteenth-century furniture outside Germany. Finally in 1976 Judge Untermyer's bequest capped his many gifts of superlative pieces from the fifteenth to the eighteenth century, which raise the Museum's English representation from mediocre to the best outside England. In the vastness of the Metropolitan Museum one can forget that the collections of the decorative arts, if detached, would make a famous museum all by themselves.

The unmatched feature of the decorative arts is the series of furnished period rooms, evocative settings of life in many places and centuries. One's exploration begins in the stone chamber of the Egyptian temple from Dendur; continues with the painted Pompeian bedroom; the glazed mosaics of 1354 in the prayer niche from Isfahan; the intarsia study of simulated cabinets from the palace of Gubbio about 1480; the airy marble patio carved by Italians at Velez Blanco in Spain about 1515, given by George Blumenthal; the rich shadowy chapel from La Bastie d'Urfey, paneled with intarsia designed by Vignola, given by the children of Mrs. Harry Payne Whitney; the gilded grille that took nearly a century to spin across the nave of Valladolid Cathedral, the gift of the Hearst Foundation; the thick acanthus branches carved in the 1670s on the stair from Cassiobury Park; the intricate snug room, with its comforting tile stove, from Canton Flims in Switzerland; the tall dim reception chamber of 1707 from Damascus, cooled by a marble floor and whispering water, given by the Kevorkian Fund; the operatic bedroom from Palazzo Sagredo on the Grand Canal in Venice, where 32 putti fly away with the fringed canopy ceiling; Lorenz Melchior's gift of choir stalls from Trier Cathedral inlaid in the 1720s with shimmering rarities as a background for seductive nude angels; the festive endless mirrors of the Hôtel de Varengeville in Paris, given and furnished, with other splendid rooms, by Mr. and Mrs. Charles Wrightsman; the extravagant drawing room from Croome Court, "papered" and upholstered with Boucher tapestries, the gift of the Kress Foundation; the grand Adam dining room rescued from the destruction of Lansdowne

12

House; the only Rococo shop front surviving ٨om Paris, sparkling with Catherine Wentworth's extraordinary silver; the intimate bathroom from the Hôtel de Crillon on the Place de la Concorde, painted with slender flowers, the gift of Susan Dwight Bliss; and to end the *ancien régime*, Mrs. Herbert N. Straus' gift of an oval room from Bordeaux, still in its original soft green paint. The nineteenth-century styles of revival will be included in the American Wing's continuous series of rooms from about 1670 to 1920. Where else can one step in and out of so much history?

Of the Metropolitan's seven directors, the first three important ones—Cesnola, Robinson and Winlock—were archaeologists who secured the first great acquisitions. In 1874 and 1876 the Museum bought Cesnola's finds from Cyprus; in 1875 Samuel Ward gave good Attic vases; in 1881 John T. Johnston gave excellent engraved gems. The Metropolitan's unique wealth of ancient glass is based on the gifts of two collections, from H. G. Marquand in 1881 and J. Pierpont Morgan, Jr. in 1917. In 1903 the new Rogers Fund paid for two superb purchases—the only grand Roman frescoes that have ever left Italy, some already 100 years old when the ashes of Vesuvius preserved them in A.D. 79 (page 39), and the only large Etruscan tomb hoard that was ever exported intact, including a sculptured ceremonial chariot. In 1908 came the marble of the old market woman (page 35). Several purchases assembled an archaic Greek grave monument, with much of its original paint. In 1927 the Museum bought the touching tombstone of a girl with doves (page 34), and in 1932 the archaic giant marble of a youth (page 32), in 1943 the bronze *Sleeping Eros* (page 36), in 1952 the most sensitive version of the Aphrodite of the Medici type (page 37). The collection is also rich in gems and amber, gold jewelry, Attic gravestones of the fourth century, and Roman bronze and marble portraits. The pottery presents a continuous series from Minoan to late Roman times, and includes work by many of the great Athenians. The most famous piece is the calyx-krater painted by Euphronios (page 33).

The other great archaeological collection, the Egyptian, comes mainly from the Museum's excavations. In 1907 Albert M. Lithgoe began to dig for the Metropolitan, first at Lisht, then at the Kharga Oasis for Coptic things, finally settling at Luxor until 1936. Edward S. Harness, who financed much of the excavation, bought the mastaba tomb of Pernebi and moved it from Saqqara to the Metropolitan, where it forms the dramatic entrance to the Egyptian galleries. In 1920 Lithgoe's successor, Herbert Winlock, discovered the vivid models of daily life on the estate of Mekutra from about 2,000 B.C. The Metropolitan's share shows a slaughter house, a cow barn, a brewery and bakery, a walled garden with trees and a pool, and a flotilla of six boats for the Nile. The department is especially rich in small objects, 1,100 being bequeathed by Theodore M. Davis from his own excavations in Egypt (page 22), and the superb collection of Lord Carnarvon, given in 1926 by Harkness. At various times the Museum has bought some of the most exquisite jewelry that has survived from any age. But the latest notable acquisition is the temple of Dendur, dismantled before the flooding of the High Dam, and given by the Egyptian Government. The present curator, Christine Lilyquist, has arranged the collection in the most instructive sequence of Egyptian art to be found anywhere.

The Museum's excavations have also contributed greatly to the latest of the archaeological departments, that of the Ancient Near East, formed in 1942. In 1930 John D. Rockefeller, Jr. had already given large reliefs and two colossal statues of Assur-nasirpal as a bull and as a lion from his palace at Nimrud. By sharing in recent British excavations in another part of Nimrud the Metropolitan acquired a fine series of ivories. Remarkable works made in Persia and Mesopotamia have come by purchase, including the exquisite metalwork illustrated on page 26 to 28.

The story begun in the ancient Near East continues in Islamic art, whose decorative mastery and diffidence toward the human body have long attracted Americans. In 1891 Edward C. Moore bequeathed outstanding pottery, metalwork and the largest series of enameled mosque lamps outside Cairo. What amounts to a comprehensive survey of Near Eastern manuscripts and miniatures of all kinds, largely given by many donors, was recently capped by Arthur A. Houghton's gift of a portion of the sumptuous *Shah nameh* illustrated in Tabriz by the best Persian painters of the early 1500s. Turkish carpets were given by James S. Ballard and extraordinary rugs of all kinds by Joseph V. McMullan. The Museum acquired the monumental incense burner shaped like a lion and two Hapsburg treasures—the sixteenth-century Persian carpet from Schonbrunn, a gift from the Kress Foundation, and the glass bottle shown on page 44. The Metropolitan's excavations at Nishapur brought in elaborate wall decorations of carved and painted stucco and pottery of a type almost unknown until then. In 1975 the collection was pulled together in a series of spectacular galleries that revealed the unequalled spread and variety of the Museum's holdings.

Ever since the clipper ship trade showed us that we face two oceans, the art of the Far East has fascinated Americans. Already in 1879, 1,300 Chinese porcelains were bought by public subscription for a collection that has become very great through the gifts of J. P. Morgan in 1902, Benjamin Altman in 1913, Samuel T. Peters in 1926, and John D. Rockefeller, Jr. in 1960. In 1887 a Chinese diplomat, Chang Yen Hoon, gave the first Han bronze for a collection that now features a shrine of gilded flames, cast in 524, and an altar set of no less than 14 pieces. In 1902 Heber R. Bishop gave over 1,000 jades of all periods. The Japanese section, which includes fine wood sculptures and screens, was greatly augmented by the purchase of a large collection in 1976. Beginning with the curatorship of S. C. Bosch-Reitz in 1915 the Museum purchased monumental Chinese sculptures until they can now be seen in greater variety at the Metropolitan than in any other single place.

Both the Near and Far East have contributed to the textile collection through Japanese and Chinese court and theatrical costumes and Islamic silks. In 1888 John Jacob Astor's gift of his late wife's lace started one of the very great lace collections. Today the Metropolitan's 30,000 textiles, if considered with those in the nearby Cooper-Hewitt Museum of Design, cover all periods and all places.

The Textile Study Room supplements the Costume Institute, founded by Irene Lewisohn in 1937, that now helps dress designers serving New York's most powerful industry. When the Costume Institute moved into the Metropolitan in 1946 it became the chief department to fulfill the clause in the Museum's charter "for the application of arts to manufacture." Its quarters were recently rebuilt to create ideal conditions for conserving and exhibiting some 30,000 items of historic costume, for providing designers with private study rooms, and a library. The dramatically staged exhibitions notably influence American fashions.

Two other departments are also devoted to objects of a particular use, the larger one being the Department of Arms and Armor. In 1904 Rutherford Stuyvesant, the Museum's trustee and an ardent collector of armor, used the new Rogers Fund to secure the historic De Dino collection in Paris. In 1912 the new Department of Arms and Armor got its first curator, the protean Bashford Dean, who was already curator of fishes in the American Museum of Natural History across the Park. In 1913 Dean's erudition, energy and tact persuaded William H. Riggs to give the collection that he had been tracking down during 60 years of rummaging in Europe. Riggs wisely asked that his gift be merged with the armor already in the Metropolitan "so that the Museum's exhibit of arms and armor should illustrate in an unbroken series all the stages of the armorer's art." Riggs' gift and subsequent astute purchases have realized this ideal with a chronological sequence like no other in its range and variety.

14 The third collection devoted to a particular use is that of musical instruments. This was mainly

created by one woman, Anne Crosby Brown, who from 1889 to 1907 developed one of the most comprehensive collections of musical instruments from all periods and all parts of the world. Among the many rarities is the earliest extant piano, constructed in Florence in 1720 by its inventor, Bartolommeo Cristofori. In 1971 the collection was rearranged in six galleries named for André Mertens, where the visitor with earphones hears recordings as he approaches each showcase.

The Metropolitan has always attracted much of its public through special exhibitions. Those assembled out of its own collections have repeatedly demonstrated the matchless spread of its holdings in glass, jewelry, furniture, tapestries and other things. Of the shows borrowed from outside, the most influential one opened in 1909 to celebrate Henry Hudson's exploration of the Hudson River in 1609 and Robert Fulton's start of steam navigation there in 1809. The Hudson-Fulton Exhibition gathered the first showing of Dutch paintings outside Europe, which attracted American collectors to the Netherlands. It also pioneered by presenting early American furniture, paintings and applied arts in order, in the Museum president's words, "to test out the question whether American art was worthy of a place in an art museum." The response was so enthusiastic that Mrs. Russell Sage gave some 600 pieces of early New England oak and pine furniture. The president, Robert W. De Forest and his friends then searched out more furnishings as well as rooms from American houses built between about 1670 and 1820. He himself had the 1822 marble façade of the U.S. Branch Bank moved from Wall Street to build onto a wing of old rooms cleverly fitted together in chronological sequence. When the American Wing opened in 1924 it at once became the Metropolitan's most imitated feature. This wing is now being enlarged to continue the display of American art and life up to Frank Lloyd Wright. Furnished rooms of various periods will alternate with museum galleries for the extensive collection of painting and sculpture.

An exhibition that opened the Metropolitan to another new realm was held in 1969 when the Museum of Primitve Art, founded by Nelson A. Rockefeller in 1956, showed its treasures with compelling drama. This great collection, given by many donors, has become a department of the Metropolitan and will be shown in a new wing named for Governor Rockefeller's son Michael, who cared deeply for primitive art. For years the Metropolitan had previously bought and been given some 4,000 "primitive" objects in its early days, but feeling that they belonged to ethnology, had lent them to other museums. Today, after Picasso and Matisse have assimilated "primitive" art into our ancestry, the new department extends the Metropolitan's collections to the latest work in which we have learned to discern subtlety and inspiration.

The Metropolitan Museum's unique diversity merely reflects the unique diversity of races that generates America's energy. Along with the whole country, the Metropolitan is ever on its way, never arriving. The Metropolitan, like the Museum of Modern Art, has time and again set the example for museums elsewhere. Yet as a whole, both museums are inimitable in their display of things that can no longer be collected and in the multiplicity of their services. But their greatest treasure has always been the devotion of the people who support and run them.

A. Hyatt Mayor

ANCIENT EGYPT
ANCIENT NEAR EAST

PREDYNASTIC PERIOD. *Gerzean jar with red figures.*

One of the finest Predynastic objects in the Museum's vast holdings of Egyptian art—the largest and most complete collection in the United States—is this vessel which can be dated to the Gerzean Period, ca. 3400–3200 B.C. The design on this so-called "decorated" vessel is typical of the lively scenes painted on pottery of Upper (Southern) Egypt in the Late Predynastic Period, when writing was in the act of being invented. Most of the elements of these designs are recognizable—mountains, wavy "water-lines," boats with cabins flying standards, trees, a sail or shield and, as on the vessel above, figures engaged in some ceremony. Nevertheless, the meaning remains obscure.

These boats are apparently drawn up on land, supported by their oars, which are extended over the gunwales, but there is no crew to man them. In order to understand such scenes without the help of a *written* description, the viewer must already have been acquainted with the concept that inspired them as well as the particular activity within that concept that is being illustrated.

MIDDLE KINGDOM. *King Senwosret I striding.*

Made up of no less than sixteen pieces of cedar skillfully joined together this figure of Senwosret I depicts him advancing forward, wearing the red crown of

MIDDLE KINGDOM
Eleventh, Twelfth and Thirteenth Dynasties,
ca. 2134—ca. 1700 B.C.
King Senwosret I striding (1972–1928 B.C.)
Painted cedar, and stucco; h. 23".
From Lisht, South Pyramid.
Found in a secret chamber in the wall around
the tomb of Senwosret's High Priest of Heli-
opolis, Imhotep.
14.3.17
Edward S. Harkness and Rogers Funds, 1914

Detail left
PREDYNASTIC PERIOD
Ca. 4000—ca. 3100 B.C.
Gerzean jar with red figures (3400–3200 B.C.)
Pottery, painted with red on buff; H. 11 13/16",
diam. 11 13/16"
Provenance unknown
20.2.10
Rogers Fund, 1920

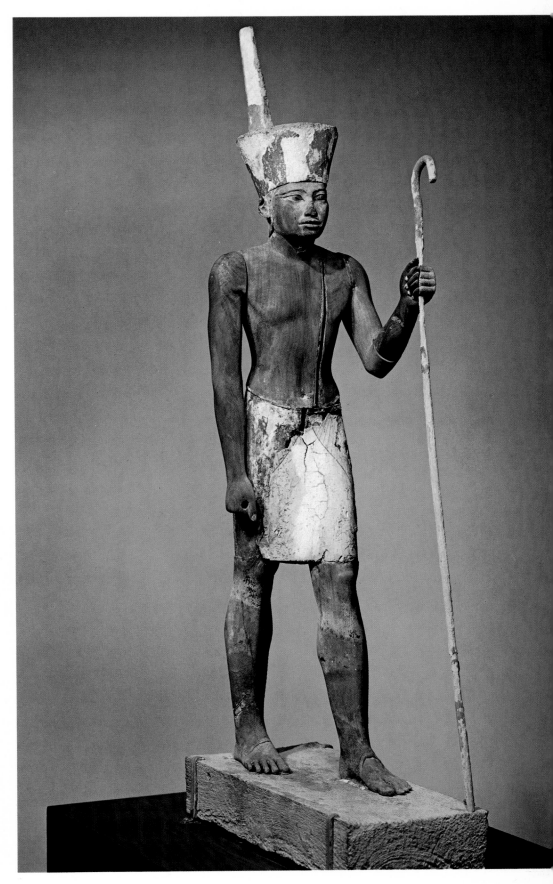

Lower Egypt and a short kilt, and holding the *ḥk3* scepter in his left hand.

This statue, which is a good example of the art of the Middle Kingdom, *projects* an aura of majesty and restrained energy. Although subject to the rules of the Egyptian tradition in art, i.e. carved to be viewed only from the front, this figure shows beautiful modeling and a very careful attention to details, which is rarely seen even in larger sculptures in the round.

Senwosret I, the second king of the XIIth Dynasty, was one of the greatest rulers of Ancient Egypt. He ascended to the throne after quashing an attempted coup d'état in which his father, Amenemhat I, was assassinated. Senwosret I enlarged the boundary of Egypt beyond the Third Cataract in Nubia, re-established the central control of the Pharaoh all over the land, and continued the renaissance of the arts—architecture, sculpture, painting and writing—during the Early Middle Kingdom.

NEW KINGDOM. *General Haremhab as a Scribe.*

Haremhab, the commoner who became a king and restored the religious beliefs to their traditional ways in the aftermath of the Amarna Period, is depicted in this statue as a scribe. The statue, which is believed to have come from the Temple of Ptah at Memphis, is a member of a group of figures carved in Memphis at the last era of the Eighteenth Dynasty. The meticulous care given to details of the flowing civil wig, the pleated skirt with its frontal apron and the flaring sleeves, together with the naturalistic rendering of the flabby belly and sagging chest bear the influences of the Amarna tradition.

The figure appears to pose in a pensive and reflective mood, in accordance with the art tradition of the period, and totally unrelated to the scribal attitude in which it is depicted.

The figure as shown is a typical example of the Memphitic school during and after the Amarna Period. It incorporates the naturalism and moodiness of Amarna with the traditional idealization of the human figure, and the meticulous attention to details, which was the trademark of Memphis.

NEW KINGDOM. *Princess Meritaten.* *p. 22*

This canopic jar head, which was excavated in a tomb in the Valley of the Kings, is identified as Princess Meritaten, eldest daughter of King Akhenaten, who married the Pharaoh Smenkhkara and was his queen. The face is done in the Late Amarna style, in which there is a softening of the gross exaggerations of the Early Amarna Period. The artist combined here all the dominant traits of his period—naturalistic features, sharp contrast in colors between the white alabaster and the dark inlays, and a clever use of the canopic jar lid as an imitation of human shoulders.

20 The Amarna Period, to which the canopic jar head of Princess Meritaten be-

NEW KINGDOM
Eighteenth Dynasty, 1570–1320 B.C.
General Haremhab as a Scribe (ca. 1355 B.C.)
Diorite; h. 46″.
The inscriptions on the statue include Haremhab's titles among which are: Commander in Chief of the Army, Deputy of the King in Front of the Two Lands; and the traditional vow of piety about helping the poor and suppressing lawlessness.
From the Temple of Ptah at Memphis.
23.10.1
Gift of Mr. and Mrs. V. Everit Macy, 1923

longs, is in many ways a watershed in the history of Egypt. The young Pharaoh, Akhenaten broke all tradition by building a capital city, Akhetaten (modern el-Amarna) at a site which had *no* previous history. Thus, starting new, he created a center for the ancient sun god *Aten,* and in a sort of Proto-monotheism, gave supremacy for Aten over all the other Egyptian gods and their ancient cities—Amun of Thebes, Ra of Heliopolis, Ptah of Memphis—and sought to create a centralized religion in Egypt, based upon the Aten as the Chief God and the Pharaoh as his representative on Earth.

NEW KINGDOM.   *Queen Hatshepsut Seated.*
Hatshepsut, the female Pharaoh, is very well represented in the Metropolitan Museum of Art's collection. This seated statue, done in indurated limestone, is one of the best examples of the sculpture in her time. The Pharaoh is uniquely depicted as a woman with delicate facial features, slim body and small breasts.

NEW KINGDOM
Eighteenth Dynasty, ca. 1570–1320 B.C.
Princess Meritaten (ca. 1365 B.C.)
Alabaster; eyes and eyebrows inlaid; h. 7".
30.8.54
Bequest of Theodore M. Davis, 1915

NEW KINGDOM
Eighteenth Dynasty, ca. 1570–1320 B.C.
Queen Hatshepsut seated (ca. 1495 B.C.)
White indurated limestone; h. 6'5".
A seated statue of the Queen, wearing the royal headdress *(nemes)* and Uraeus. Traces of paint are noticeable on the headdress, eyes and eyebrows, the broad collar and the inscriptions.
From the Mortuary Temple of Hatshepsut, Deir el-Bahri, Western Thebes.
29.3.2
Rogers Fund, 1926–28

Her attitude and her attire are those traditionally used in the representations of royal figures.

The statue, though heavily restored, is a magnificent example of the Theban art tradition at the beginning of the Eighteenth Dynasty.

Hatshepsut, one of Egypt's female rulers, lived during a period of Egyptian ascendancy. Her father, Thutmosis I, was the first Egyptian ruler to campaign into Mesopotamia and her nephew, Thutmosis III, who succeeded her to the throne, established the first Egyptian empire in Asia.

IRAN. *Head of a Man.*

IRAN
Late third millennium B.C.
Head of a Man
Bronze, eyes originally inlaid; h. 13½".
Reputedly from Teppé Tikhon, northwest Iran.
47.100.80
Rogers Fund, 1947

This bronze head of a ruler from Iran was formerly attributed to the late second millennium B.C., but recent research places its origin a thousand years earlier, toward the end of the third millennium B.C. The main reason for this change is its resemblance in certain details to the Old Akkadian head from Nineveh, now in the Iraq Museum. In addition, an analysis of the metal reveals that it is arsenical rather than tin bronze. Since tin bronze generally replaces arsenical bronze near the close of the third millennium B.C., the arsenical bronze supports the earlier date.

That the sculpture does not closely resemble typical heads from either Iran or Mesopotamia possibly means that it portrays an individual ruler, a ruler whose name we may never know.

IRAN. *Gazelle Cup.* p. 26

This exquisite golden cup is thought to have come from the area of "Amlash," southwest of the Caspian Sea, in Iran, the home of a remarkably rich variety of ancient works of art. Raised from a single sheet of gold, it is decorated with four striding gazelles, whose heads turn out from the cup. Each head was made separately and then was expertly joined to the neck by a hard-soldering process. Ears and horns were subsequently added—the horns, rolled from a single piece of flat gold, rise elegantly above the flattened rim of the cup. The bodies of the four animals, raised in low relief on the side of the vessel, are decorated by chased marks indicating both the body hair and the stylized patterns of the legs. It is evident from the naturalistic modelling of the animals that the artist knew the form of the gazelle exceedingly well. Ancient Near Eastern, and especially Iranian, sculptors always seem to have possessed a sensitive knowledge of animal forms.

The animals are framed by a complex double guilloche pattern at the top of the cup and by a single guilloche band near the bottom. Beneath this band the cup expands into an inflated base ring, characteristic of related metal vessels excavated in the Amlash region and dating to around 1000 B.C. On the underside of the cup six interlocking rosettes are arrayed against a dotted background and are enclosed in circles drawn by a compass.

Whatever the purpose of the vessel—a votive offering or a royal drinking cup—its precious material and superb workmanship ensures that it will always be among the treasures of ancient Iranian art.

24

IRAN, SASANIAN PERIOD. *Head of a King.*

This nearly life-size head raised from a single sheet of silver is the most extraordinary example preserved to us of the imagery of kings that dominated the art of the Near East during the Sasanian period. The identity of the silver king, although not certain, is probably Shapur II who from 399–420 A.D. ruled the vast Sasanian empire which extended from Afghanistan in the east to Syria and even to Egypt in the west.

The king wears a gilded crenellated crown bordered with beading. Above the crown rises a large vertically ribbed globe with concentric circle decoration at its top. His hair curls back in four rows of raised locks; his long mustache flows outward and full beard downward ending in a braid tied with a bow. His wide-open eyes stare directly forward, commanding complete attention of the beholder.

It is impossible to know if this silver head of a king was part of a complete statue or if it was used alone as a royal bust. But there can be no doubt that it embodied the awesome power of an omnipotent monarch.

IRAN, SASANIAN PERIOD
Ca. 4th century A.D.
Head of a King
Silver with mercury gilding; 15 3/8″ x 9 1/16″.
65.125
Fletcher Fund, 1965

IRAN, ACHAEMENIAN PERIOD.
Rhyton in the form of a lion griffin. p. 28

This Achaemenian drinking horn is a masterpiece of goldsmithing, from the inventive conceptual form of a fantastic lion-griffin to the execution of fine details, such as the individual teeth, protruding tongue, and sharp nails of the paws. The rhyton is in the basic form of a lion with extended forelegs, and its

IRAN
Ca. 1000 B.C.
Gazelle Cup
Gold, the bodies of the gazelles in repoussé, the heads in the round, details chased; h. 2 9/16″, diam. 3 3/8″.
From Guilan, northwest Iran.
62.84
Rogers Fund, 1962

griffin attributes include the head crest and a wing on each of its flanks. The body of the animal loses its identity as it bends sharply upwards at a right angle and rises into the slightly taller drinking horn. Below the rim of the horn lie forty-four rows of extremely fine, double-twisted gold wires. The lion-griffin protome is hollow, and is sealed off from the horn by a separate, small gold cup secured within the body of the protome. The royal drink, in this way, would have been poured into the horn, as well as drunk from it. The rhyton is composed of a number of individual parts, each having been formed by hammering, then decorated by the techniques of repoussé and chasing, and finally thermally joined. The distinguishing Achaemenian stylistic conventions include the irregular, figure-eight shoulder muscle, the tulip-shaped muscle on each foreleg, and the overall pattern of tiny tufts of fur fitting close to the body.

IRAN, ACHAEMENIAN PERIOD
Ca. 5th century B.C.
Rhyton in the form of a lion-griffin
Gold; h. 6 3/4", diam. (mouth) 5½".
54.3.3
Fletcher Fund, 1954

ANCIENT GREECE
ANCIENT ROME

GEOMETRIC PERIOD. *Bronze Horse.*

Reduced to basic structure and essential lines, with an esthetic freedom as great as today's, this little archaic sculpture shows that bronze-working flourished at the same time as vase-painting during the period that is commonly called Geometric. Although human figures were made as well, animals were particularly favored and have come to light in great number both in Northern Greece and in the Peloponnesus, at sanctuary sites like Olympia.

The design of the bronze illustrates with what skill simple forms were composed into an expressive composition. The fretwork on the base of the horse suggests the rhythmic marks of the animal's hooves. The clear line of the back joins the corresponding curves of the neck, hind legs and tail, and is balanced by the curve of the chest.

The remarkable range of form and mastery of proportion in what was probably a votive object shows the level of esthetic refinement in Greece in the eighth century B.C.

GEOMETRIC PERIOD
8th century B.C.
Bronze Horse
H. 6 15/16", length 5¼".
21.88.24
Rogers Fund, 1921

30

EARLY CYCLADIC PERIOD
Ca. 3000—2700 B.C.
Seated Harp Player
Marble; h. 11½".
47.100.1
Rogers Fund, 1947

EARLY CYCLADIC PERIOD. *Seated Harp Player.* *p. 31*

Hundreds of marble statuettes have been found in the Aegean Islands documenting a flourishing culture that goes back to the fourth millennium B.C. This work (of a type known in other variants) is one of the most complex and elaborate in design and workmanship. The heavy lyre, the unusual presence of a high-backed chair, the harpist's solid body, are combined so as to create a masterful sense of clarity and order without sacrificing the volume of the human figure. The function, or purpose, of the work remains unknown, though like the great majority of Cycladic statuettes and vases, it probably came to light in a grave. In any case, it shows that over two thousand years before the time of Homer, the musician—if not the bard—was already an important figure.

ARCHAIC PERIOD. *Statue of a Youth (Kouros).*

As one of the oldest surviving marble sculptures from Attica, this statue sheds light upon the relationship between Egyptian sculpture and early Greek monumental works in stone.

The kouros shares with Egyptian sculpture its cubic form entailing strict frontality and the "scissors" stance of the legs. The figure is, however, entirely freestanding, each limb is modelled separately, and bones and muscles are articulated not only to animate the surface but especially to suggest the potential for movement. The result is a clear departure from Egyptian prototypes.

During the late seventh and sixth centuries, statues like this one were used as grave monuments or offered as dedications.

ARCHAIC PERIOD. *Neck Amphora: Marriage Procession.* *p. 33, left*

The art of Greek vase-painting reached its greatest heights in Athens between the late seventh and fourth centuries B.C. This vase was made about 540 B.C. and is decorated in a technique (black-figure) whereby the figures and ornament are drawn upon the clay surface and embellished with incision and added color. The main scene shows a couple in a chariot, who may form part of a marriage procession. The narrow frieze on the shoulder depicts a battle. The spirals below the handles and the zones of pattern work serve as frames to the pictures while they also emphasize the various parts of the shape. The artist, Exekias, was one of the great masters who not only painted vases but also made them.

ARCHAIC PERIOD. *Calyx-krater: The Death of Sarpedon.* *p. 33, right*

Around 530 B.C. a new technique (red-figure) was introduced to Attic vase-painting; the decoration now remained the color of the clay surface while the background was filled in. The new procedure allowed the painter to draw more freely; he could show his figures in more complicated postures and articulate them more fully. One of the first artists to exploit these possibilities was Euphronios, who painted the krater for the potter Euxitheos.

The subject is taken from the Iliad. The body of Sarpedon, a Trojan hero and son of the god Apollo, is being lifted from the battlefield by Sleep and Death, who will carry him to his native Lycia for burial. By focusing on the impressive figure of Sarpedon and by juxtaposing the realm of gods and heroes with that of the two mortals standing at each side, Euphronios has created a forceful and memorable image.

ARCHAIC PERIOD
Statue of a Youth (Kouros)
Marble; h. 6'4".
Attic style, late 7th century B.C.
32.11.1
Fletcher Fund, 1932

Below
ARCHAIC PERIOD
Neck amphora: Marriage Procession
Attic, ca. 540 B.C.
Black figure technique; h. 18 ½".
Exekias, to whom this amphora is attributed,
was both potter and painter.
From the Thomas Hope Collection.
17.230.14
Rogers Fund, 1917

Right
ARCHAIC PERIOD
Calyx-krater: The Death of Sarpedon
Attic, 520–510 B.C.
Red-figure technique with additions of opaque
red; h. 18"; diameter 21 11/16". Signed by
Exitheos as potter and Euphronios as painter.
An inscription praising the young Leagros helps
date the krater in the last decade of the 6th cen-
tury.
1972. 11.10
Bequest of Joseph H. Durkee, Gift of Darius
Ogden Mills, and Gift of Mr. and Mrs. C. Rux-
ton Love, by exchange, 1972

CLASSICAL PERIOD. *Grave stele: A girl with doves.* p. 34
A delicate young girl shown clasping two doves appears on a grave stele discovered during the eighteenth century at Liatani on the Cycladic island of Paros, most probably the place for which it was originally intended. In this memo-
rial, the sculptor has combined the body of a child with the ideal head of a
young woman. Her features and elaborate hairstyle reflect the style of the
sculptor Polykleitos. Further inspiration was drawn from the east frieze of the
Parthenon, which exerted a profound influence on sculptors, as well as artists
in other media, active during the second half of the fifth century. The poignan-
cy of the representation here is due to the contrast between the body, an image
of the dead child, and the head portraying the woman that the child never grew
to be. The execution of the two parts differs as well. The head is soft, with a
full face and particular emphasis on the wavy, flowing hair. The garment is
treated more broadly, and appears somewhat stiff with its highly pleated vertical folds. Though a touching detail, the doves are little more than a decorative
motif.

HELLENISTIC PERIOD. *Old Market Woman.* p. 35
The peasant woman, straining under the weight of the produce she is carrying
to market—chickens and a basket of vegetables and fruit—clearly illustrates
the profound change that overcame Greek art during the three centuries of ex-

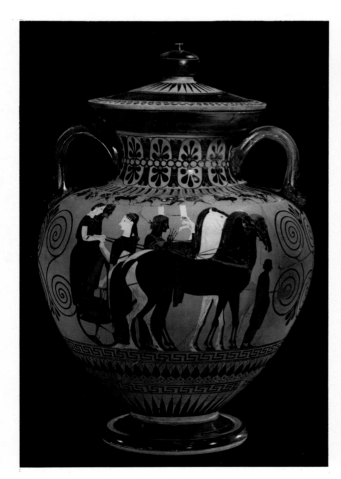

pansion, foreign contacts, and transformation that mark the Hellenistic period (323–31 B.C.). The "noble simplicity and quiet grandeur" that had characterized classical Greek art of the fifth and fourth centuries gave way to a taste for the personal, the immediate, the dramatic.

Visibly worn by fatigue and age, the woman is rendered realistically yet sympathetically, so that she retains a certain dignity. At the same time, the sculptor

CLASSICAL PERIOD
Grave stele: A girl with doves
Ca. 450 B.C.
Parian marble: 31½″ x 15 3/8″.
Found on the island of Paros in 1775.
Formerly in the collection of the Earls of Yarborough, Brocklesby Park, England.
27.45
Fletcher Fund, 1927

HELLENISTIC PERIOD
Old Market Woman
Marble; h. 49½".
2nd century B.C.
Found in Rome.
09.39
Rogers Fund, 1909

was clearly concerned with the play of drapery over her body, and the effects of light and texture he could achieve. The work is among the most significant and stylistically most accomplished examples of a Hellenism that may stem from Asia Minor.

HELLENISTIC PERIOD. *Sleeping Eros.*

Eros, the young attendant of Aphrodite, began to be truly popular in Greek art during the fifth century B.C. It was in the Hellenistic period, however, that the characterization of Eros developed from that of a small youthful person with wings into that of a child. This work illustrates the achievement admirably. A young boy with a soft fleshy body is shown lying on a base (remade in stone) in a position in which only a child can sleep. His wings alone distinguish him from an ordinary mortal. The immediacy and naturalism of the rendering depends to a great extent in the technical mastery that bronze workers had acquired by the third century B.C. The sculpture was cast by the "lost wax process" in six

HELLENISTIC PERIOD
Sleeping Eros
Bronze; length 33 9/16".
3rd century B.C.
Said to be from the Island of Rhodes.
43.11.4
Rogers Fund, 1943

AUGUSTAN PERIOD
Aphrodite
Marble; h. with plinth 5′ 2½″.
Augustan copy of a Greek original of about 300
B.C., based on the same source as the Medici
Venus. The legs from below the knees to the
ankles are plaster casts of the Medici Venus.
Successively in the collections of Count Schla-
brendorf (friend of Winckelmann), Count Cha-
mare, and Countless Edith Strachwitz.
52.11.5
Fletcher Fund, 1952

pieces (including the left arm, now missing) that were then carefully joined. Equally accomplished was the cold-working of surface detail in the boy's hair and wings. Though often overshadowed by its more stark and brutal manifestation, Hellenistic art also produced fresh and engaging works, of which this is surely one of the most notable.

AUGUSTAN PERIOD. *Aphrodite.* p. 37
In early Greek art, the male body was shown nude, the female body virtually always draped. One of the major innovations of the classical period was the introduction of the nude female body, and in the statue of Aphrodite made for the island of Knidos, Praxiteles for the first time represented the goddess without drapery. This celebrated work of ca. 350 B.C., as well as the variations to which it gave rise, are known to us through Roman copies. The original of the Metropolitan *Aphrodite* was made about 300 B.C.

The goddess here is to be imagined at her bath; the dolphin refers to her miraculous emergence from the sea. The effect of the sculpture depends considerably on the highly polished marble of which it is made and the play of light created by the graceful torsion in her pose.

POMPEIAN. *Kithara Player.*
This figure formed part of the mural decoration in a villa at Boscoreale, situated on the foothills of Mount Vesuvius and destroyed by the eruption of A.D. 79 that overwhelmed Pompeii and Herculaneum.

The painting is one of three in the Museum from the same room; none of the subjects, however, have been conclusively explained. Here, in any case, we see a Roman lady richly dressed and bejewelled, seated in a throne-like chair with a young girl behind. She holds a kithara, but seems more intent on something before her than on her instrument. The sumptuous effect of the painting is created not only by the subject, but also by the rich and luminous colors that are well preserved. Given the dearth of ancient painting preserved to us, such Roman frescoes are as important to us as they are beautiful.

ETRUSCAN. *Finial from a candelabrum:*
Warrior giving support to a wounded comrade. p. 40
From the late eighth century on, the Etruscans became increasingly familiar with Greek art both through the Greek colonies that were established in Italy and especially through the objects that were imported directly from Greece. Though they drew heavily on these models for subject matter, for instance,

POMPEIAN
Kithara Player
Painted on plaster; 6' 1½" x 6' 1½".
Ca. 40–30 B.C.
From the east wall of a large room in a villa near Boscoreale, buried by the eruption of the Vesuvius in A.D. 79. Two other paintings from the west wall are in the National Museum, Naples.
03.14.5
Rogers Fund, 1903

Etruscan artists nonetheless developed styles and specialties very much their own. From early times, the Etruscans were consummate metal workers, as proven by their gold and silver jewelry as well as bronze sculptures like this one.

In Etruscan as in Greek art, human or animal figures often served as decorative adjuncts to utilitarian objects; the present piece was the finial of a lampstand. It shows two warriors, one of whom has been wounded and is being supported by his comrade. The subject is an exceedingly personal and human one for an article of household furniture, but this is one of the hallmarks of classical works of art. Moreover, the artist has achieved here a wholly satisfactory three-dimensional group as well as a characterization of the two different but interdependent personalities.

ETRUSCAN
Finial from a candelabrum: Warrior giving support to a wounded comrad
Early 5th century B.C.
Bronze; h. (with base) 5 ¼".
Already known in Italy in the 18th century. Later in the collection of the Duke of Buccleuch.
47.11.3
Rogers Fund, 1947

40

IRAN
ISLAM

SELJUQ. *Dish with seated musician.*

The conquest of the Islamic lands by the Seljuq tribes beginning in 1038 brought active signs of technical and formal renewal in every field of representational art. Similar to the work from Rayy, this wide bowl or dish of the so-called *"minai"* type, dating from the late twelfth or early thirteenth century, has the characteristic monochrome turquoise ground often used. Of special interest is the setting for the principal figure, here achieved with great effect by the insertion of two bowls of fruit, a real "still life." The decoration of the wide border is also typical, in the recurrent motif of ovals and stylized plant forms aligned between two slender bands, enclosing various little seated figures acting as if in a chorus for the central figure, a woman playing a musical instrument which has been identified as a member of the lute family. *Minai* is the Persian word for enamel, in a process in which stable colors were stain-painted in the glaze and fired, then less stable colors applied and the object re-fired at a lower temperature.

SELJUQ. *Bowl with ruler surrounded by attendants.* p. 43

Trials and experiments in the field of ceramics led the Iranian craftsmen of the thirteenth century to superb accomplishments, technical as well as artistic. The reflections of light and the delicate harmony of colors combine to create works

SELJUQ
Kashan, 13th century
Bowl with ruler surrounded by attendants
Lustre-painted composite body; h. 7″., diam. 14 ⅞″.
41.199.1
Gift of Horace Havemeyer, 1941

SELJUQ
Late 12th—early 13th century
Dish with seated musician
Overglaze polychromy and gilt on turquoise glaze; h. 3½″, diam. 7 ¾″.
Henry G. Leberthon Collection.
57.61.16
Gift of Mr. and Mrs. A. Wallace Chauncey, 1957

SYRIAN
Mamluk period, first half of 14th century
Bottle
Enameled and gilt glass; h. 17 ⅛".
Chinese phoenix on neck; frieze of fighting warriors on horseback, on body.
41.150
Rogers Fund, 1941

SELJUQ
Kashan, 13th century
Openwork Ewer
Pierced and glazed composite body entirely covered with transparent turquoise blue glaze; in two parts, the outer pierced and decorated in blue and black; h. 8".
Inscribed at rim and below the pierced decoration, and dated 612 A.H. (A.D. 1215/16).
From the collection of V. Everit Macy.
32.52.1
Fletcher Fund, 1932

of the greatest refinement, like this dish from Kashan, which bears the exact date it was made, November-December 1210.

The rhythmic vertical cadence of the human figures on a ground of arabesques—always dear to the Seljuq masters—has a new fluency; the human figure is used as a basic motif and the numerous bystanders are arranged in uninterrupted lines, on either side of and behind the figure in front, while the sumptuous robes (and the central throne, with the two little surrounding patterns of olive branches above and fish below) is assigned the function of continuing the arabesque decoration. Art Nouveau adopted many of these stylistic devices from Persian art.

SYRIAN. *Bottle.* *p. 44*

During the long domination of the Mamluks (1250–1517) in Syria and Egypt, the artistic activity that flourished there was particularly distinguished in the field of what are rather arbitrarily called the "minor arts" which, thanks to the remarkable skill of the master glaziers, the carvers in wood and ivory, and the workers in plaster and metal, were raised to a superlative level. In the crowded ornamentation, where arabesques and palm-leaves are intertwined with geometric motifs, there are also naturalistic motifs, evidently derived from the neighboring production of the Mongols, who established themselves in Iran in the same period (1256–1393).

The Mongolian relationship is particularly evident in the wide band of horsemen that surrounds the lower body of this stupendous glass bottle, and in the band around the neck which depicts a Phoenix, with the exquisite flowing movement of its feathers.

But the creator of this *tour de force* has not overlooked motifs nearest and most familiar to the Mamluk tradition, namely the four medallions crowded with arabesques on the upper part of the body which are placed amid a composed, ordered pattern of gilded ribbons mingled with fields of flowers. From the lowest blue band around the conical neck to the line above the horsemen comprising the upper part of the body—an area equal in height with the lower, supporting part—and also in the division of space between the medallions and the background fields of that area, and even in the composition of the battle scene, there is a foundation of discipline which gives complete harmony to this work of supreme beauty, a real masterpiece of Syrian art.

SELJUQ. *Openwork Ewer.*

This jug dated 1215–16, from the city of Kashan in Iran, is a perfect example of Persian ceramics from the time of the Seljuqs. It shows how the Islamic artists of the period exploited every possible motif for decoration, whether individually or in combination—arabesques and inscriptions, human figures, fish, birds, animals, leaves, water—all masterfully stylized and worked into a dense pattern of refined and fascinating delicacy.

But this jug adds even further to this profusion of decorative patterns by superimposing open-work ornament over the monochrome ewer like a second skin.

CENTRAL ASIAN. *Four demons.*

This extraordinary painting on silk is reminiscent of the group of paintings associated with the name Master Muhammad Siyah Qalem, or Black Pen. Several of them, found in albums, at one time called The Albums of Mehmet the Conqueror, which are preserved in the Topkapi Serayi Palace library in Istanbul, are ascribed to this unknown artist.

While they vary in quality and date, suggesting different artists and a continuing tradition, they form a cohesive group which takes its imagery from the nomadic culture of the Asian steppe. Most of the paintings, however imaginary the subjects of some of them, are rendered with extraordinary realism and vigor. The underlying linear quality of the style was no doubt responsible for the nickname Siyal Qalem, or Black Pen.

While fine wash drawings on silk, as here, were influenced by Chinese painting—which must also have provided some of the models for the demons and strange beasts—and while the subjects reflect a central Asian nomadic milieu, the paintings may well have been produced in Iran for patrons fascinated by this aspect of their heritage.

CENTRAL ASIAN
15th century
Four Demons
Colors and gilt, on silk; greatest length 13 ⅜",
greatest width 7 15/16.
68.175
Harris Brisbane Dick Fund, 1968

PERSIAN. *Majnun with the black dog outside Layla's camp.*   *p. 47, left*

While the calligrapher Ala ad-Din Muhammad of Herat copied this now dis-

46

Below
PERSIAN
Probably Herat School, 1520–1525
Majnun with the black dog outside Layla's camp
Miniature, 8½" x 5¼".
Sheet from a dispersed manuscript of the Khamseh of Amir Khosrou Dihlavi.
13.160,3
Rogers Fund, 1913

Right
SAFAVID
Northwest Persia, probably Tabriz, early 16th century
Compartment rug, detail
Silk warp, silk weft, wool pile;
16'4" x 11'2".
10.61.3
Frederick C. Hewitt Fund, 1910

persed manuscript at Balkh, the miniatures were most likely painted in Herat, as their style is still in the tradition of the school headed by the famous miniaturist, Bihzad.

The page illustrated depicts the introduction to the story of the tender and tragic love of Layla and Majnun who, after overcoming earthly misfortunes, were to be joined in heaven only after their death. Substantially influenced by the great tradition of fifteenth-century Timurid painting, the scenes and figures are idealized with a delicacy of drawing, a harmonious composition of figures, and elements of landscape and architecture set in areas of pure color in a style that is close to the work of Bihzad. Little polychrome dots mark the detail of a garment, a face, the ground, sketched with a fluid elegance that is found also in the written sections above and below the miniatures. The calligraphy, an elegant

example of Nasta'liq script, is placed in four columns, with a most delicate pattern of curves and points.

SAFAVID. *Compartment rug*, detail. *p. 47, right*

Closely related to the painting and miniatures of the time are the rugs of the Safavid period in Iran (ca. 1500–1737). These are characterized by a series of motifs—either animal or human—grouped around a central dominant element, composed with wonderful rhythmic cadences on a ground of arabesques and framed by borders, which in turn are elaborations of the same motifs—lovely frames for the beautiful themes they enclose.

The layout of these masterpieces of pictorial art is extremely varied, not only according to the different purposes for which the rug is intended but also in the diversity of the basic motifs chosen. Compartment rugs, like this one, are made up of heterogeneous elements put together in various ways but without any single element predominating, such as the superb "heraldic" medallions in this example, with monsters and birds against a spidery web of plant forms on different colored grounds. However, the deep and more uniform frame of the border, which repeats the design of the medallions between long, dark cartouches of unusual length, tends to acquire greater importance than the central part, vibrating with the curves of the plant forms in the foreground, and pausing between the rhythms of changing form, color, size and decoration in the medallions.

INDIA
INDONESIA
CHINA
JAPAN

CHINA: NORTHERN WEI DYNASTY. *Maitreya.*   *p. 51, left*

Buddhism, a religion founded in India in the sixth and fifth centuries B.C., slowly spread to Central Asia and eventually reached China about the first century A.D. It became firmly rooted in China under the T'o-pa, a Hsien-pi Tartar people who invaded and ruled north China as the Northern Wei dynasty from 386-535 A.D. Many Northern Wei emperors were fervent Buddhists and actively encouraged Buddhism. In 460 A.D. Emperor Wen-ch'eng ordered the carving of the greatest monument of early Buddhist art in China: the cave temples of Yün-kang in Shansi province, near the capital Ta-t'ung.

For close to forty years, thousands upon thousands of sculptors and craftsmen labored to hew a vast complex of some twenty major cave temples out of the sandstone mountain ridge of Yün-kang, under the shadow of the Great Wall. Each of the five earliest caves contains a colossal image of Buddha, the tallest measuring over fifty feet in height, filling almost the entire excavation; while the later caves are more architectural in concept with intricate ground plans and walls arranged in several stories. The interior walls of the caves were carved into niches and galleries filled with images of Buddhas, Bodhisattvas, apsaras or celestial musicians, donors and guardians.

This image from Yün-kang probably once graced in niche in Cave XVA. It represents Maitreya, or Mi-lo-fo in Chinese, the Buddha of the Future who will descend from the Tushita Heaven to save all living creatures. His true right hand is in the *abhaya mudra,* signifying "fear not"; while his left hand is in the *varada mudra,* a gesture denoting charity.

The broadly rendered sculpture, with a serene and spiritual face and a body carved in a flat and slender manner, is conceived as an abstract diamond pattern with the tall crown as the apex and the knees and crossed ankles as the other cardinal points.

Originally many of the sculptures at Yün-kang were brightly painted with polychrome. Traces of red and white pigments remain on the lower portion of the piece, giving added warmth to this superb icon.

CHINA: NORTHERN WEI DYNASTY
Late 5th century
Maitreya
Stone with traces of polychromy; h. 51".
148.162.2
Gift of Robert Lehman, 1948

NORTHERN INDIA. *Standing Buddha.*   *p. 51, right*

Dating from the late Gupta period, this image is stylistically dependent on types developed in Madhya Pradesh and Uttar Pradesh (Central and North Central India) during the sixth century.

The sculptural styles of the great Gupta empire are well preserved by rich remains in stone, but relatively few bronzes have survived. When the esthetic qualities of a surviving bronze sculpture are on a particularly high level, its importance is considerably enhanced.

Here, the Buddha stands in a slight hip-shot position, his left hand holding a portion of his outer robe; his right, raised in the fear-allaying gesture, clearly shows the webbing between the fingers, one of the supranatural physical marks of a Buddha. This tall and elegant image with its large, powerful head is the kind of North Indian sculpture that played a major role in the formulation of the early Nepali style. Indeed, part of the long history of this particular sculpture included a stay of unknown duration in Nepal.

NORTHERN INDIA
First half of 7th century
Standing Buddha
Bronze; h. 18½".
69.222
Bequest of Florance Waterbury, 1969

THAILAND
Mon-Dvaravati period, ca. second quarter of 8th century
Four-armed Avalokiteshvara
Bronze, eyes inlaid with silver and black glass or obsidian; h. 56″.
67.234
Rogers Fund, 1967

CAMBODIA
Angkor period, Baphuon style, ca. mid-11th century
Kneeling Queen
Bronze with traces of gold, eyes inlaid with silver; h. 17″.
1972.147
Bequest of Joseph H. Durkee, by exchange, 1972

THAILAND. *Four-armed Avalokiteshvara.* *p. 52, left*

In 1964, a remarkable group of Buddhist bronzes was accidentally discovered at Pra Kon Chai in Buriram Province, Thailand. These sculptures reflect clear Cambodian, Indian and Thai influences in an unequal admixture, with the contribution of the Mon-Dvaravati styles of Thailand apparent in the physiognomy and treatment of the body. Their stylistic affiliations with Shri Deb and Lopburi, major centers for sculpture production in central Thailand, help to localize the style of most of these sculptures.

Almost no bronzes of comparable size and early date have survived from India. This reflects historical accident rather than an accurate account of the history of bronze casting in India. The discovery of the Pra Kon Chai trove caused the rewriting of the early art history of Thailand. Since these sculptures are mature products of important workshops it is likely that more of their type must have been made and perhaps exported throughout Southeast Asia. These have either all been melted down or are awaiting another serendipitous discovery.

The Metropolitan Museum's *Avalokiteshvara, Lord of Infinite Compassion,* identifiable through the small Buddha Amitabha in the hairdo, is the largest and one of the finest of the bronzes from the Pra Kon Chai treasure trove.

CHINA: CH'ING DYNASTY
Late 17th–early 18th century, probably K'ang-hsi period
God of Wealth in his Civil Aspect (?)
Porcelain painted in polychrome enamels (*famille verte*) on the biscuit; H. 23 ⅞".
61.200.11
Bequest of John D. Rockefeller, Jr., 1960

CAMBODIA: ANGKOR PERIOD. *Kneeling Queen.* *p. 52, right*

This regal female is superbly modeled in soft generalized forms, with a surface made taut as if by an inner expanding energy. The composition of the figure suggests an organic expansion, the narrow contour of the legs, hips and waist blossoming to full shoulders supporting a large head framed by the raised arms.

Strong but harmonious visual rhythms and contrasts of form are established by the sharp, diamond-shaped silhouette of the raised arms and the graceful arrangement of the masses of the lower part of the body. The upward visual thrust of the hands has its counterpart in the thrust of the right knee toward the spectator. Altogether this is a magnificently poised and balanced sculpture, successfully conceived from every viewing angle.

The "Queen" wears a pleated *sarong* secured by a sash with jeweled pendents. The left hem of the *sarong* is folded over, creating a frontal panel of cloth resting between the legs and terminating in the "fishtail" silhouette reminiscent of earlier Khmer styles. The precision of detail of jewelry, dress, and hairdo shows a particularly high level of metalworking technique, surely the work of a major imperial workshop.

The statue dates to around the middle of the eleventh century, and is in the style of the Baphuon temple (ca. 1010–1080), which can be considered the "classic" phase of Khmer architecture and sculpture, rooted in the transitional style of Banteay Srei (ca. 967–1000) and contrasting strongly with the more iconic art of the ninth and first half of the tenth centuries.

CHINA: CH'ING DYNASTY. *God of Wealth* p. 53

Among the most striking porcelains of the K'ang-hsi period are those decorated in the palette of enamels which goes by the name of *famille verte*. These brightly colored and translucent enamels—in which several shades of green are almost invariably present (and hence the name)—are applied rather heavily over dark outlines and details. Here used to embellish a splendidly modelled statue of the God of Wealth in his Civil Aspect, the enamels have been applied to the pre-fired porcelain body (known as "enameling on the biscuit"), and re-fired at a lower temperature. The resplendence of the figure is matched by his filagreed hat set with pearls, jade and kingfisher feathers and the gilded silver throne from which he reigns.

CHINA: SUNG DYNASTY. *Tribute Horse.*

Combining an aristocratically decorative realism in the execution of figures with a complex, illusionistic treatment of the natural scenery, *The Tribute Horse* presents a mixture of the conservative T'ang figure painting tradition with the Sung's advances in the description of landscape that may well belong to the late eleventh or early twelfth century. Possibly once part of a folding

CHINA: SUNG DYNASTY
960–1280 A.D.
Tribute Horse
Colors on silk; 32 ⅝" x 44 ⅞".
41.138
Rogers Fund, 1941

54

JAPAN: KAMAKURA PERIOD
Life of Prince Shotoku
Colors on silk; 67⅝" x 33¼".
First half of 14th century.
29.100.470
Bequest of Mrs. H.O. Havemeyer, 1929
The H.O. Havemeyer Collection

screen, a format transitional between the ancient mural art and the "modern" handscroll, this painting belongs to the tradition of narrative illustration.

While identification of the "story" here is not certain, the subject is believed to be the T'ang Emperor Ming-huang's flight to Szechwan during the rebellion of An Lu-shan in 756 A.D.; specifically, the cheerless journey after the death of his favorite consort Yang Kuei-fei at the hands of his mutinous army. Escorting a riderless white horse, this richly colored procession winds its way through a brooding mountainscape where foothills glow an eerie gold.

KAMAKURA PERIOD.   *Life of Prince Shotoku Taishi*, detail.
This detail is from a pictorial biography in 62 scenes memorializing one of Japan's first great culture heroes, Shotoku Taishi—Crown Prince "Saintly Virtue." Born around A.D. 574, he served as regent during the reign of the widowed Empress Suiko, a time of rapid political change that saw the introduction of a centralized system of government modeled on China's. He was a devout champion of the newly imported Buddhist religion, which he made the religion of the court and fostered by building a number of important temples, notably the Horyuji at Nara, which still stands. By the medieval period—from which this scroll dates—Shotoku had become the focus of a popular cult which revered him as a savior deity, an incarnation of the Guze Kannon.

The cult was based on an early tenth-century hagiography, the *Shotoku Taishi Denreki*, written by a Kyoto court official. A pictorial biography predated even

55

this, and the earliest extant example of this type is the series of ten large silk paintings executed in A.D. 1069 for the walls of the "Painting Hall" in the Horyuji temple. From the thirteenth and fourteenth centuries, there survive a large number of such representations. In this painting, the compact arrangement of a multitude of small-scale scenes with realistic settings precisely drawn and brightly colored is typical of the narrative hanging scrolls popular in this period.

JAPAN: EDO PERIOD.   *Trees and Flowers by a Stream.*

As early as the mid-eighth century an anthology of poetry, *Manyoshu,* mentions flowers and trees, which in the Japanese mind denote specific seasons. This subtle connection between flora and the seasons has for centuries been a part of the Japanese artist's repertoire. In this screen—one of a pair on the Four Seasons—the mood of spring is created by light-colored blossoms of *yamabuki,* pear, cherry and iris, and accented with tiny red azalea blossoms. Thus, the feeling of the season is conveyed not with one but with several spring plants. The river running behind the pine trees and through blossoms creates the feeling of a balmy spring day.

The pines trees in the center overlapping the river project a certain amount of realism and suggest depth. Yet some abstraction is still displayed in this painting: massive open space, big clumps of pine leaves and stylized waves are conceived in a style reflecting the influence of Sotatsu (first half of the seventeenth century) and Kōrin (1658–1716).

The screen bears neither signature nor seal. Although Fenollosa and some others considered this pair of screens to be original works of Kōetsu (1558–1637), modern scholars discredit this attribution. However, no single artist has yet been named.

JAPAN: EDO PERIOD
Sotatsu-Korin School, 17th century
Trees and Flowers by a Stream
Color on mounted paper; 48″ x 123″.
One of a pair of 6-fold screens on the "Four Seasons," the companion of which had been acquired by the Museum 34 years earlier.
49.35.2
Gift of Horace Havemeyer, 1949.

AFRICA
OCEANIA
PRE-COLUMBIAN AMERICA

PRE-COLUMBIAN ART: PERU. *Storage Containers.*

Nathan Cummings has recently presented a fine pair of storage jars to the Metropolitan Museum to add to the outstanding collection of Peruvian pottery previously donated. The top part of these large jars is incised and painted with trophy head demons typical of the late Paracas style. The two jars, said to be from the site of Chucho below the Pisco River drainage, are examples of the magnificent flowering of so-called Rio Grande pottery tradition which in the period between 300 and 100 BC established itself as the richest and most original forms of production on the south coast of Peru. These jars are of exceptional interest in that they have survived centuries of burial intact. They are identical in shape, size and decoration. The only difference is the nubbin which is the relief head of a falcon, its unfurled wings painted on the body of the jar.

OCEANIC ART: PAPUA NEW GUINEA. *Mask.* *p. 59, left*

Papua New Guinea—the eastern half of the island New Guinea—is famous for its traditions of mask-making. A wide variety of materials is used, from such impermanent substances as unbaked clay, gourd, and bark-cloth to longer-lasting basketry and carved wood. They represent generally spirits of the water and the forest, sometimes embodied as mythical ancestors. Their uses also vary considerably: in some areas important masks are kept in the men's cere-

PRE-COLUMBIAN ART: PERU
300–100 B.C.
Storage containers
Resin-painted clay blackware, with upper surfaces in colored pigment; painted bird-figures have three-dimensional heads; h. 17½", w. 16 15/16".
1974.173.2
Gift of Nathan Cummings, 1974

Below
OCEANIC ART: PAPUA NEW GUINEA
Mask
Carved and painted wood; h. 15 15/16″, w. 6 ⅜″.
Style of the Rao Tribe, Guam River area.
Collected in the Madang Province.
1975.305
Morgan and Rogers Funds, 1975

Right
PRE-COLUMBIAN ART: COLOMBIA
14-16th centuries
Figural pendant
Gold; h. 5¼″, w. 6½″.
69.7.10
Gift of H.L. Bache Foundation, 1969

monial houses as secret objects of great spiritual power displayed only on ritual occasions to initiates. Others are worn publicly, usually attached to elaborate costumes with splendid decorations of shell ornaments, flowers, leaves and feathers. The mask illustrated is one of the latter. It comes from the Ramu River valley, an area close to the Sepik River valley (which is well-known as the most productive area of art in the country), and shares a number of characteristics of masks from the mouth of the Sepik. It is probably from the Rao tribe, a little-known group of the middle Ramu River.

PRE-COLUMBIAN ART: COLOMBIA. *Figural Pendant.*
The metalwork of Colombia played an important part in the lively and fruitful interchange between ancient South American civilizations. We do not yet know the full extent of Colombia's contribution to ancient South American civilization, but its metalwork was fascinating, and richly varied in output and may be regarded as unique of its kind. In the northeast, the peoples of the Sierra Nevada de Santa Marta formed a distinct cultural entity and this highly sophisticated pendant is a superb example of its so-called "Tairona" style (A.D. 1200-1500). The figure with its enormous headdress is one of several which share like features. The frontal figures hold similar objects (here rattle-like) in each hand, and the large headdresses consist of lateral spirals and paired stylized profile bird and animal heads. From the visor of the figures' caps there are pairs of long-beaked bird heads. Representational differences among the

figures are in the details of the face, nose rods, lip plugs, and ear ornaments, are variable. A major distinction, however, occurs when the figure appears with a crocodile head. As in many other Pre-Columbian cultures, the Tairona alloyed gold with copper, and many of these elaborate works were cast in that alloy. Some of the most impressive work of the ancient American goldsmith was done by the Tairona.

AFRICAN ART: MALI.   *Staff with seated figure.*

This seated male figure, cast in bronze by the lost wax method, surmounts a thick, forged iron staff. Little is known about the function this staff may have served. The large size, luxury of the material, and the refinement of the workmanship suggest that it must have belonged to a person of high rank. It may have been used like other metal-tipped staffs found in Africa which are thrust into the ground to stand upright during ceremonial occasions.

Because it is distinct in style and one of the most elaborate, naturalistic, and fully conceived bronzes we know from Mali, this piece is difficult to attribute. An early date has been suggested but cannot be confirmed by scientific methods. The rounded treatment of the body, the prominent ribs and breasts and the tubular limbs as well as elements of the regalia can be found in Dogon wood sculpture, but the naturalism of the face and the subject of a seated, crowned figure are unique in Malian art.

PRE-COLUMBIAN ART: MEXICO.   *Seated Standard-bearer.*   *p. 61*

In 1903, during a journey to Veracruz, Eduard Seler discovered this imposing figure (holding in its damaged right hand the shaft of a plumed standard) in the town hall at Castillo de Teayo in the Mexican state of Veracruz. Probably one of a pair, it originally stood at the top of a pyramid flanking the stairway. Remains of the pyramid survive, now in the middle of the town which began to grow around it in the 1870s. Castillo de Teayo was anciently a small town established by the Aztecs during the fifteenth century when they extended their rule into Veracruz. The figure is a late work, done at a time when Aztec sculptors had absorbed the artistic forms and traditions of the various people that they had conquered. Here they were clearly influenced by the Toltecs. Traditional elements are fused with the magical and spontaneously vital quality (there is a sense of repressed energy in the large, resting figure) characteristic of Aztec sculpture in general. This is exemplified in the stern strength of this figure, the simultaneous view of all its planes, internal and external, and in its compact three-dimensional quality and angled composition.

AFRICAN ART: NIGERIA.   *Saltcellar.*   *p. 62*

This vessel is one of a small number of works known today as Afro-Portuguese ivories because they were commissioned by Portuguese travellers from African artists. Made in the early sixteenth century, they represent the earliest and most successful instance of outside cultural influence upon African art. The subject—a knight and his attendant—is strictly European, but it is seen through African eyes. The saltcellar was carved according to African techniques, specifically those of the Igbesamwan guild of carvers at the court of Benin.

PRE-COLUMBIAN ART: MEXICO
Aztec, late 15th century
Seated standard bearer (ca. 1480–1491)
Laminated sandstone; h. 31 ⅝", w. 13 ⅜".
62.47
Harris Brisbane Dick Fund, 1962

AFRICAN ART: MALI
Staff with seated figure, detail
Bronze and iron; h. 30".
Dogon style.
1975.306
Morgan and Rogers Funds

Faithful to the variety of patterns and *horror vacui* aesthetic of the Benin court tradition, the Bini artist has represented in careful detail those features of his exotic foreign visitors that he found most arresting: their complicated garments, hose, and shoes, their pointed noses and emphatically straight-haired beards. Other alien things such as the necklace with a cross and the key hanging at the attendant's waist have also been closely observed.

AFRICAN ART: NIGERIA
Early 16th century
Saltcellar
Ivory, double vessel in two tiers;
h. 7⅛", w. 3".
Bini-Portuguese style.
1972.63
Bell and Rogers Fund, 1972

ITALY

GIOTTO. *Nativity and Adoration.*
This panel is one of a series on the *Life of Christ* of which six others survive:
The Presentation in the Temple (Boston, Isabella Stewart Gardner Museum),
The Last Supper, Crucifixion and *Christ in Limbo* (Munich, Alte Pinakothek),
The Entombment (Settignano, Berenson Collection), and *The Pentecost* (London, National Gallery). This series is related stylistically to Giotto's frescoes in
the Peruzzi chapel in Santa Croce, Florence, and it has been suggested that the
scenes were part of a set of panels for the altar of that chapel or for the adjoining Bardi chapel. According to another theory these scenes from the *Life of
Christ* may have been part of an altarpiece in Borgo San Sepolcro, which Vasari reports was dismembered and subsequently brought to Florence in the fourteenth century.

This group of almost square panels, if completed by other scenes usually included in such traditional treatments of the *Life of Christ* as the decorations of
the Arena chapel, might have numbered as many as twenty-four. If divided into
two sets they might have constituted the doors of the kind of cupboards one often finds in church sacristies. In the surviving seven pictures, Giotto, now in his
full maturity, reduces the plastic forms to essentials and creates a subtly balanced composition of monumental masses.

SASSETTA. *The Journey of the Magi.*   *p. 66*
This is undoubtedly the upper right-hand fragment of a larger composition. The
main part, an *Adoration of the Magi,* is now in the Chigi-Saraceni Collection in
Siena. The gold star that is at the lower right of the Metropolitan's fragment
would have been directly over the head of the Christ Child in the Adoration
scene when the painting was intact.

The removal of this fragment from the much larger work showing the ritual
homage of the three wise men has not affected the composition to any great extent, since the two scenes—although related—seem to have been conceived independently. The balanced rhythm of the opposing slopes gives the cavalcade
of small figures the quality of a charming, picturesque fable.

SASSETTA. *Temptation of St. Anthony Abbot.*   *p. 67*
This is one of the panels of a predella which together with seven other scenes
depicting the life of St. Anthony—in museums in Berlin (1), Washington (4),
and Yale (2)—was clearly part of a polyptych dedicated to the saint. Two
works have been put forward as the central panel of this polyptych, the *St. Anthony Abbot in Meditation* in the Louvre and another one in a private collection
in Genoa. Yet the major pieces of the work remain unknown or in question, as

GIOTTO DI BONDONE
Colle di Vespignano 1267(?)—Florence 1337
*Nativity, Adoration of the Shepherds and the
Magi*
Tempera on wood, gold ground; 17 ¾″ x 17¼″.
11.126.1
John Stewart Kennedy Fund, 1911

is its original destination. There is also controversy about its authorship. In fact it has been suggested that it was not Sassetta, but a painter known as the Osservanza Master, who worked in the same accentuated, linear Gothic style. The old saint is walking along a stony road in a landscape swept by the freezing wind, the bare trees appearing like black skeletons. In paintings such as these, the artist—who in other works uses Florentine perspective—prefers a freedom of vision which allows him the maximum amount of fantasy not tied to realism.

GIOVANNI DI PAOLO. *Expulsion from Paradise.* p. 68
This extraordinary work in the Lehman Collection has assured the Metropolitan Museum of a second fragment of the predella that formed part of the polyptych probably painted for the Church of San Domenico in Siena. The Almighty, descending supported by cherubs, points out the cosmography of the Earth, which is encircled by iridescent celestial spheres and contains the signs of the Zodiac within its external rim. Nearby the Archangel drives Adam and Eve

SASSETTA (STEFANO DI GIOVANNI)
Asciano 1392(?)—Siena 1450/1451
The Journey of the Magi
Tempera on wood; 8½″ x 11⅝″.
43.98.1
Bequest of Maitland Fuller Griggs, 1943

from the earthly paradise after their sin. This is an unrealistic vision, where the diagonal descent of the divine figures, supported by numerous wings, sets in motion the rhythmic, dancing steps of the figures running counter to the line of flowering trees.

GIOVANNI DI PAOLO. *Paradise.* *p. 69*

This work, cut down on the right-hand side, is probably part of the predella of an as yet unidentified altarpiece which would have been combined with scenes of the Last Judgment and Hell. It is unanimously dated about 1445, when the artist was at the height of his powers. According to the most widely held belief

SASSETTA (STEFANO DI GIOVANNI)
Asciano 1392(?)—Siena 1450/1451
Temptation of St. Anthony Abbot
Tempera on panel; 18 ⅝″ x 13½″.
Previously in the collection of Prince
Leon Ourousoff, Vienna.
Robert Lehman Collection, 1975

GIOVANNI DI PAOLO
Siena 1403—Siena 1482
Expulsion from Paradise (ca. 1445)
Tempera on panel; 17 15/16″ x 20½″.
Robert Lehman Collection, 1975

it was part of the altarpiece painted in 1445 for the Guelfi Chapel of the church of San Domenico in Siena.

It is clear that we are dealing with a commemoration of the Dominican Order, as is shown by the presence of St. Dominic—who embraces St. Peter Martyr—of St. Thomas Aquinas and of various Dominican monks and nuns. In the peace of the celestial garden, ardent mystics—for example Abelard and Heloïse, St. Augustine and St. Catherine of Siena—welcomed and led by slender, golden-winged angels, meet and embrace joyfully in a meadow of rare plants and precious flowers, beneath a network of golden-leaved trees.

Giovanni di Paolo returned to this subject much later in his predella panels of *Paradise,* the *Last Judgment,* and *Hell* in the Pinacoteca, Siena.

VECCHIETTA. *St. Bernardino Preaching.* *p. 70*
The subject commemorates two famous sermons preached by St. Bernardino Albizzeschi in Siena in 1425, in the piazza of San Francesco and the Campo. A

GIOVANNI DI PAOLO
Siena 1403—Siena 1482
Paradise
Tempera on canvas, transferred from wood; 18½ x 16.
06.1046
Rogers Fund, 1906

close contemporary, Sano di Pietro, recorded the scene in two descriptive and topographically accurate paintings in the chapter of Siena Cathedral. The fact that there is no halo in this fine miniature has cast doubt on the identity of the subject though his appearance seems to confirm that he is St. Bernardino. However it has been suggested that the solitary preacher may be the famous Giovanni da Capistrano who was not canonized until the seventeenth century.

The artist clearly intended this picture to be an unusually vivid and immediate vision taken from life, as evidenced by the figure's stance and appearance and by the bare improvised pulpit of wooden planks, a stark and straightforward geometrical shape. Compared with the many other often more formal religious paintings of St. Bernardino which have survived, this small, worn, expressive portrait of the preacher calmly and eloquently making his point is an extraordinarily moving work.

The miniature is attributed to Vecchietta and this is plausible if we take into account other examples of his work which are not stylized and formal in scope, but concerned with revealing the joyful side of Franciscan life.

VECCHIETTA (LORENZO DI PIETRO)
Castiglione di Val d'Orcia ca. 1405—1412–1480
St. Bernardino of Siena Preaching
Independent miniature; 8¼" x 5½".
Signed on verso: *Ferrarie fecit Laurentius Vecchietta*.
Robert Lehman Collection, 1975.

FILIPPO LIPPI
Florence ca. 1406—Spoleto 1469
Madonna and Child
Tempera, with gold halos, on wood, transferred from the original panel; 48¼" x 24¾".
49.7.9
The Jules Bache Collection, 1949

The Madonna and Child Enthroned
FRA FILIPPO LIPPI
ITALIAN, 1406?–1469
THE JULES S. BACHE COLLECTION, 1949

AVE MARIA GRASIA PLENA DOS TECO

FILIPPO LIPPI. *Madonna and Child.*   *p. 71*

This painting from the Bache Collection was the central part of a triptych; the wings, representing the four *Fathers of the Church*, are in the Galleria dell'Accademia Albertina in Turin. It is quite possible that it was originally joined with the other panels in a composition comparable to the *Madonna with Saints* for the church of Santo Spirito now in the Louvre. The Madonna, seated on a polychromed marble throne, is flanked by angels, one of whom holds a scroll inscribed with verses from the Apocrypha.

Impressed at the beginning of his career by the works of Masaccio and Paolo Uccello, Lippi established his own style with the *Madonna Enthroned* of Cor-

ANDREA MANTEGNA
Isola di Carturo 1431—Mantua 1506
Adoration of the Shepherds
Tempera on canvas, transferred from wood;
15¾" x 21⅞".
From the collection of Clarence H. Mackay,
Roslyn, Long Island, N.Y.
32.130.2
Anonymous gift, 1932

neto Tarquinia of 1437, a direct antecedent of the work in the Metropolitan Museum. The Bache Collection *Madonna* can be dated between 1437 and 1444.

ANDREA MANTEGNA.   *Adoration of the Shepherds.*   *p. 72*
This was certainly part of a predella though its origin and relevant details are not known. Two drawings relating to this painting have survived in the Uffizi (*Madonna*) and Windsor Castle (*Shepherds*). In this *Adoration*, sculptured rock formations echo the composition of the statue-like figures, which are conceived and represented in sharp relief, as if worked in metal. The enamel-like forms and the tense, wiry lines are characteristic of Mantegna's early work and this

GIOVANNI BELLINI
Venice ca. 1430—Venice 1516
Madonna and Child (ca. 1460)
Tempera on panel; 21 5/16″ x 15⅝″
Formerly in the collection of the Potenziani princes, of Rieti and the Marches.
Robert Lehman Collection, 1975.

painting, which may come from Ferrara, dates from before 1460, the year of the altarpiece for San Zeno in Verona.

GIOVANNI BELLINI. *Madonna and Child.*   *p. 73*

The Potenziani Madonna (so-called because of its provenance) is qualitatively one of the greatest testaments to Bellini's youthful period. The light, shafting in from the left, gives form, life and vibration to the static group in the foreground and highlights the deep colors, as well as the suspended green garland, which forms a small inner framework within which the figures are shown as though in high relief, carved out of hard, precious materials. In the arrangement and modelling of its three-dimensional forms, the work clearly shows its debt to the contemporary master of Padua, Andrea Mantegna. And this is also true of the landscape, stretching some way behind the Madonna's shoulders; it spreads out in marked contrast in the depths of the background up to the wide sweep of the river. Compared with Mantegna's stony, archeological impassivity, Bellini's *Madonna*—dated about 1460—communicates a penetrating and emotional intensity.

MASTER OF THE BARBERINI PANELS. *Birth of the Virgin.*

The companion piece, depicting the *Presentation of the Virgin in the Temple,* also belonged formerly to the Barberini collection in Rome and was acquired by the Museum of Fine Arts, Boston, in 1937. The presence of the three arches at the top of each panel may indicate that they were fixed to the wall of a room. The architectural discontinuity of the two scenes, except in the lower part, suggests that there was a section in between, perhaps with a central focal point, whereas the perspective in these two scenes is divergent. They are, however, definitely related and interdependent, and may come from the Ducal Palace in Urbino (the eagles painted on the ornamental shields on the main arch may be the arms of the Duke of Montefeltro).

There has been much argument about the authorship of the two panels, which have been linked to other works, for example an *Annunication* in Washington. They were painted by an artist who was influenced by Filippo Lippi, Domenico Veneziano and Piero della Francesca, and whose work has something in common with that of Giovanni Boccati. The painter was keenly interested in classical architectural motifs—note for example the use of the Ionic order and the reliefs with pagan themes—and may also have known the work of Leon Battista Alberti. He has been tentatively identified as Giovanni Angelo da Camerino, a colleague of Boccati, who worked in Florence for a member of the Medici family in 1451.

MASTER OF THE BARBERINI PANELS
(GIOVANNI ANGELO DI ANTONIO DA CAMERINO)
School of the Marches, active ca. 1447—ca. 1475
Birth of the Virgin
Oil and tempera on wood; 57 x 37⅞".
35.121
Rogers and Gwynne Andrews Funds, 1935

ANDREA DEL VERROCCHIO.   *Madonna and Child.*

From the early fifteenth century the workshops of even the greatest Italian sculptors (such as Donatello and Ghiberti) produced works in cheaper materials as well as in stone and metal. Thus their Madonnas in terracotta, stucco or plaster, often painted, reached a broad audience. Often they are mere copies of compositions in more important materials, but they deserve attention because some are the sole survivors of their prototypes. This Madonna, certainly produced in the studio of Andrea del Verrocchio, is not known in any other example. It was modelled independently and not cast, but it is uncertain whether it was a preliminary model or a relatively inexpensive work of art in its own right. It has features in common with the Madonna from S. Maria Nuova (Florence, Bargello) but shows a maturer approach to anatomy.

ANDREA DEL VERROCCHIO (ANDREA DI CIONE), WORKSHOP
Florence 1435. His very active workshop of painters as well as sculptors included the young Leonardo da Vinci. Active in Florence until 1479, when he left for Venice to execute the Colleoni monument.
Died in Venice in 1488.
Madonna and Child (last quarter of the 15th century)
Terracotta polychromed and gilt; 30½ x 23 inches.
09.215
Rogers Fund, 1909

SANDRO BOTTICELLI
(ALESSANDRO FILIPEPI)
Florence 1444/45–Florence 1510
Last Communion of St. Jerome
Tempera on wood; 13½ x 10.
14.40.642
¹ Bequest of Benjamin Altman, 1913

SANDRO BOTTICELLI. *Last Communion of St. Jerome.* p. 77

In the last years of his life Botticelli painted this little panel for Francesco di Filippo del Pugliese, with whom he shared a passionate devotion to the mysticism of Savonarola. Its theme is derived from an apocryphal letter to the Blessed Eusebius, published in Florence in 1490. The picture was probably painted somewhat later, but before 1502, when it is mentioned in Pugliese's will.

In the rustic thatched cottage the tremulous Saint, who has left his bed, kneels to receive the sacrament. He is supported by two tenderly solicitous friars as the priest, attended by two acolytes, bends forward to place the Host between his parted lips.

PIERO DI COSIMO. *A Hunting Scene.*

This panel is one of a series depicting the origins of civilization, and is possibly identical with the *storie* described by Vasari as having been painted by Piero di Cosimo for a room in the house of Francesco del Pugliese. Another picture in the Metropolitan Museum, from the same series, shows the first migration of primitive man over water by boat, and a third, in the Ashmolean Museum in Oxford, represents a forest fire. From various classical sources, Piero di Cosimo found the inspiration for similarly unusual subjects: Prometheus, the battle of the Centaurs and the Lapiths, the stories of Silenus and the discovery of honey—quite obviously avoiding the biblical account of creation. Such themes of the wild and savage origins of man occur frequently in sixteenth-century German painting. The pictorial parallels with Pollaiuolo, Signorelli, and Filippino Lippi enable us to date these vividly imaginative panels around 1500.

PIERO DI COSIMO
(PIERO DI LORENZO)
Florence ca. 1462—Florence 1521
A Hunting Scene
Tempera and oil on wood; 27¾" x 66¾".
75.7.2
Gift of Robert Gordon, 1875

PIERO POLLAIUOLO. *Portrait of a Young Lady.*
The Florentine profile portrait draws on a tradition going back to the fourteenth century with precedents in antique art. As conceived by such artists as Masaccio, Uccello, Piero della Francesca, and Pollaiuolo, the profile portrait presents a silhouette against a uniform background with no indication of depth.

PIERO DEL POLLAIUOLO
(PIERO DI JACOPO BENCI)
Florence 1443—Rome 1496
Portrait of a Young Lady (ca. 1470)
Tempera on wood; 19¼" x 13⅞".
50.135.3
Bequest of Edward S. Harkness, 1940

79

The sheer force of the emerging linear contour creates a lively three-dimensional effect. Pollaiuolo's portraits, particularly the ones in Berlin and in the Poldi Pezzoli Museum in Milan, are distinguished by the similarly vibrant portrait in the Uffizi, both dating around 1475, and demonstrate with their rich, layered impasto and serpentine brush strokes a concern as well as for the tactile quality of the paint.

VITTORE CARPACCIO
Active Venice 1490 —d. 1523/26
The Meditation on the Passion
Tempera on wood; 27¾″ x 34⅛″.
Signed lower right: *vjctorjs carpattjj/ venettj opus* (legible only in infra-red photograph).
11.118
John Stewart Kennedy Fund, 1911

VITTORE CARPACCIO. *The Meditation on the Passion.* *p. 80*

This complex representation, rich in symbols alluding to the Resurrection and its meaning for human life, shows the dead Christ on a half-crumbled throne. In the foreground on either side are Job and St. Jerome (the scholarly commentator on the *Book of Job*), both portrayed as hermits. The work bears the authentic signature of Vittore Carpaccio, which was discovered some years ago under the forged signature of the Paduan master Mantegna. The craggy hills and the stratified landscape do indeed reflect the style of Mantegna, and there are echoes also of Antonello da Messina and Giovanni Bellini, all these influences pointing to a date in Carpaccio's career before the great St. Ursula cycle of about 1491. Some scholars, however, put the date after 1500. The composition is lit from two sources: one high up on the left, and one coming from the bottom left, casting strong clashing shadows. Composition and light create an intense drama, which is also reflected in the backround contrast between the mountainous, barren land behind St. Jerome and the luxuriant sun-bathed countryside behind Job.

LORENZO LOTTO. *Portrait of Gregorio da Vicenza.* *p. 82*

By means of the inscription at the bottom we can identify this painting as the portrait from the life which Lorenzo Lotto referred to in his account book on 9 December 1546 and, again, on 11 October of the following year. Fra Gregorio da Vicenza was a member of the community of the Hieronymites, who had their seat in Venice at the church and monastery of San Sebastiano.

The wild landscape and the distant Crucifixion—reminiscent perhaps of Grünewald—lit by the rays of the setting sun give this portrait a powerfully dramatic religious quality. This portrait—the intense expression, the proud, strong hands—is a fine example of the painter's characteristically subtle, psychological penetration of his subject.

TITIAN. *Venus and the Lute Player.* *p. 83*

This example of a subject so beloved by Titian was painted in his later years, around 1560, and seems to be the prototype for an almost identical version in the Fitzwilliam Museum, Cambridge.

The hypothesis that a number of years passed between the beginning and the completion of this painting is unconvincing. There is in it an evident link with the two versions of *Venus and the Organ Player*, one of which, the Prado picture, can be dated 1548 on reliable documentary evidence. This entire group is characterized by Titian's adoption of a large crescent-shaped form, which unifies the entire composition against a bold background. Other examples are the *Dresden Venus* (a work by Giorgione which Titian finished), Titian's *Venus of Urbino* of 1538, and the many others he did within a relatively short period of time at the height of his maturity as an artist.

LORENZO LOTTO
Venice ca. 1480—Loreto 1556
Portrait of Brother Gregorio da Vicenza (1547)
Oil on canvas; 34⅜″ x 28″.
Inscribed in Latin and dated: Fra Gregorio Belo
of Vicenza, hermit in the Hieronymite
Order of the Blessed Fra Pietro of Pisa, in
his 55th year, 1547.
65.117
Rogers Fund, 1965

TITIAN
Pieve di Cadore 1488-90—Venice 1576
Venus and the Lute Player
Oil on canvas; 65″ x 82½″.
36.29
Frank A. Munsey Fund, 1936

BRONZINO. *Portrait of a young man.*
This portrait was identified as a Duke of Urbino by the lengend on an old engraving by Pietro Fontana. The sitter, however, bears no resemblance to authenticated portraits of Guidobaldo II, who was Duke of Urbino at this time.

This portrait is usually dated in the 1530's, immediately following Bronzino's return to Florence from Pesaro, where he undertook several commissions for the Duke of Urbino. The portraits of a *Young Man with a Lute*, the *Bartolomeo Panciatichi* in the Uffizi and the *Ugolino Martelli* in Berlin are approximately contemporary with the Metropolitan's portrait. The striking figure stands in the center of a noble setting of an architectural interior. The diagonal composition and the general prismatic delineation show further how Bronzino was returning, like Rosso and Pontormo, to the art of the Quattrocento. The head, precisely rendered and sculptural in its modelling, goes back to the classical manner, not with sentimental nostalgia but rather in the search for aesthetic truth, the full meaning of which is proudly rediscovered in this extraordinary renewal of the ancient equation of architecture, sculpture and painting.

BRONZINO
(AGNOLO DI COSIMO DI MARIANO)
Florence 1503—Florence 1572
Portrait of a Young Man
Oil on wood; 37⅝" x 29½".
29.100.16
Bequest of Mrs. H.O. Havemeyer, 1929
The H.O. Havemeyer Collection

PAOLO VERONESE
(PAOLO CALIARI)
Verona 1528—Venice 1588
Mars and Venus United by Love
Oil and canvas; 81" x 63⅜".
Signed (on marble fragment at bottom):
PAVLVS VERONENSIS. F.
The earliest recorded owner of this painting
was Emperor Rudolf II, Prague, and then his
successor Ferdinand III; it was subsequently in
the collection of Queen Christina of Sweden;
later, the Dukes of Orléans, including Duke
Philippe d'Orléans, Paris.
10.189
John Stewart Kennedy Fund, 1910

84

PAVLVS · VERONENSIS · F

PAOLO VERONESE. *Mars and Venus united by Love.* *p. 85*

Although this painting appears to illustrate a simple fable of love it may actually be laden with complicated symbolism. This signed work dates from about 1570, when Veronese was at the height of his powers. For a long time it has been thought to have been part of a series of allegories painted for the Emperor Rudolph II in about 1576, and later in the collection of Queen Christina of Sweden. In fact, it may be from another series, mythological rather than allegorical, or perhaps an isolated work.

On several occasions, most notably in 1575, in the decorations for the Sala del Collegio of the Doge's Palace in Venice, Veronese experimented on the walls and ceiling with unusual formats, using broken, curved shapes. The scenes look fleeting and ephemeral, but their composition and perspective are firmly rooted in a knowledge of fifteenth-century proportion and measure.

This picture of Mars and Venus is rendered as a light-hearted Arcadian scene with a hint of Ariosto-like irony. Yet underlying the mood, and without destroying it, a web of structural relationships combines the figures and their setting in a brilliant, animated whole.

TINTORETTO (JACOPO ROBUSTI)
Venice 1518(?)—Venice 1594
The Finding of Moses (ca. 1570)
Oil on canvas; 30½" x 52¾".
This painting is one of the few that seems to be entirely by Tintoretto, even in the details of the background.
39.55
Gwynne Andrews Fund, 1939

TINTORETTO. *The Finding of Moses.*

The dating of this work is controversial. Some scholars regard it as relatively early, from the same period as the organ shutters for Santa Maria Zobenigo

(1557) or even earlier. Others more convincingly place it with later works from around 1570, such as the magnificent, tumultuous ceiling paintings of the Scuola di San Rocco.

Attention is concentrated on the center of the painting. The two women, clad in veil-like garments with transparent, light-catching folds, are restless, ghost-like figures forming a spiralling arch. On either side of them the onlooker's eye is drawn towards a rich, rustling landscape, with huntsmen and fishermen, small, bright figures against the wind-tossed background and troubled waters. Although fully carried out, this work of Tintoretto's has all the immediacy and dash of a sketch or first draft.

CARAVAGGIO
(MICHELANGELO MERISI)
Caravaggio 1573 —Porto Ercole 1610
The Musicians
Oil on canvas; 36¼″ x 46⅝″.
The inscription, lower left, [MI]CHELANG [ELO]DA CARAVA/[G]GIO, is a later addition.
52.81
Rogers Fund, 1952

CARAVAGGIO.   *The Musicians.*
This picture is generally identified with the painting of young musicians which Caravaggio, according to his early biographers, made for his patron, Cardinal

del Monte. It dates from about 1594, the early part of the artist's Roman period. Early writers noted the similarities between this painting and the *Lute Player*, now in the Hermitage, Leningrad. In the Metropolitan's *Musicians*, the lute is the point around which the figures are composed; the two main figures are placed diagonally face-to-face—the traditional pose in paintings of card players. The figures in the backround open out the composition, but continue its diagonal, criss-cross patterns. Reacting against contemporary Mannerism, Caravaggio turned to ancient art and to the style of the Italian Renaissance for clarity and precision of form. The pure, three-dimensional quality of the work is emphasized by the way it is lit—with a single shaft of light, falling from the left. The scene has a certain detachment and serenity, a nostalgic echo of pagan art.

GIOVANNI BATTISTA TIEPOLO.   *The Capture of Carthage*, detail.
This painting, with *The Triumph of Marius* and *The Battle of Vercellae*, also in the Metropolitan Museum, formed part of the huge decoration consisting of ten scenes from Roman history which Tiepolo painted between 1729 and 1732 for the magnificent hall of Ca' Dolfin, the seat of the Patriarch of Aquileia in Venice. Five others are now in Leningrad, and two more are in Vienna.

Together with the fresco cycle painted for the Archbishop of Udine (1726–28), this series is the most splendid of Tiepolo's early works. He drew consciously on the great dramatic tradition of Bernini, a tradition with which he was acquainted through the work of certain Neapolitan and Venetian artists. He enriched the heroic style with a handling of light and color which he learned from sixteenth-century Venetian painting, especially Paolo Veronese, who was also the inspiration for his daring use of perspective. The cycle of paintings for Ca' Dolfin, particularly the larger paintings like *The Capture of Carthage*, reveal an imagination which could shape a tumult of powerful, conflicting energies into a unified, masterly vision.

GIOVANNI BATTISTA TIEPOLO
Venice 1696—Madrid 1770
The Capture of Carthage, detail
Oil on canvas; 169½ x 148¼".
65.183.2
Rogers Fund, 1965

FRANCESCO GUARDI. *Fantastic Landscape.*

This *Fantastic Landscape*, and the two other canvases by Guardi which came to the Museum from the castle of Colloredo, are examples of the imaginary landscapes or *capriccios* so highly favored by the artist. All three take for their subjects motifs that were popular in the romantic landscape painting of the time: a classical colonnade in ruins; a tower and archway in ruins near a harbor with fishermen; and (reproduced here) a ruined tower by a lake with palm trees. The sky is the real subject of these paintings as it so often is in landscapes by the mature Guardi. The celebration of space in the three canvases shows how Guardi like an eagle longed for dominion over depths of water and sky.

FRANCESCO GUARDI
Venice 1712—Venice 1793
Fantastic Landscape
Oil on canvas; 61¼″ x 74½″.
53.225.3
Gift of Julia A. Berwind, 1953

FRANCE

JEAN DE LIÈGE. *Marie de France (?).*

This bust is believed to be part of the effigy of a funerary monument. The slightly concave back of the head seems to indicate that it rested on a pillow. Jean de Liège, a sculptor from the Meuse Valley, worked in Paris for Charles V at the same time as André Beauneveu, and when he died in 1382 he left in his studio the portraits of the two daughters of Charles IV, the Fair, and his wife Jeanne d'Evreux: Blanche, duchess of Orleans (d. 1392) and Marie of France (d. 1341). Both sisters were buried in the same tomb in Saint-Denis, destroyed with many others during the French Revolution in 1793. A series of holes on the carved head-band indicate that a metal coronet, probably decorated with jewels, enhanced the already beautiful head. It is not completely sure that the young woman is Marie because the portrait style responds to an idealized type that shows the aristocratic features common to princesses and queens of the Parisian royalty. The subtle modelling reveals the hand of a master and the smile is characteristic of the sculptures—both secular and religious—produced in Ile-de-France and imitated throughout France and in other countries.

AUVERGNE *Virgin and Child Enthroned.* *p. 93*

This oak sculpture from the mountains of Auvergne is one of a rather large group of twelfth-century carvings representing the Virgin enthroned as *"Sedes*

JEAN DE LIÈGE
Active in Paris 1361-1382
Marie de France (?), (1327-1341)
Marble; h. 12½".
From the Chapel of Notre-Dame La Blanche at Saint-Denis.
Formerly Dufay Collection, Paris
41.100.132
Gift of George Blumenthal, 1941

AUVERGNE
Second half of 12th century
Virgin and Child Enthroned
Polychromed oak; h. 31".
Formerly Georges Hoentschel and
Molinier Collections.
16.32.194
Gift of J. Pierpont Morgan, 1916

JEAN FOUQUET
Tours 1415/20—Tours 1480
Descent of the Holy Ghost upon the Faithful
(ca. 1452)
Miniature; 7 ¾″ × 5¾″.
The inscription in capital letters below contains
the first words in Latin of the Office of Vespers
prayer, "O God incline unto mine aid, Lord
make haste to help me." Within the first letter,
D, are the initials of Etienne Chevalier.
Robert Lehman Collection, 1975

sapientiae.'' With some variations in quality—enough to indicate the hand of different artists—all these sculptures respond to a common iconographic type and were produced in the same region. One of the better known, the Virgin of Orcival, is still in its original location. Others are in museums—like another one at The Cloisters Collection of the Metropolitan Museum—and several in private collections—the Tella and Coray among others.

The figure of Mary, with the Child sitting in her lap completely frontal, is massive and more geometrical than realistic. The rather flat body, dominated by the fully rounded head, is covered by tunic and mantle described by a series of parallel ridges that curve without revealing the shape underneath or giving a sense of movement. They bring to mind the treatment of the draperies in some Far Eastern sculptures. The beautiful and calm expression on Mary's face, with her eyes staring at some point beyond us, has a spellbinding quality.

JEAN FOUQUET. *Descent of the Holy Ghost upon the Faithful.*   *p. 94*

This miniature of the *Descent of the Holy Ghost upon the Faithful* was part of the Book of Hours which Jean Fouquet painted between 1450 and 1460 for Etienne Chevalier, treasurer to the French kings Charles VII and Louis XI. The precious volume was split up during the eighteenth century but fortunately forty-seven pages have survived, forty in the Musée Condé at Chantilly, two in the Louvre and one each in the Bibliothèque Nationale, Paris, the British Museum, London, the Bearsted collection, London, and the Wildenstein collection, New York.

The work has suffered some damage and oxidation, the inevitable result of its

MASTER OF MOULINS
Active last quarter of 15th to first years of 16th centuries in the court of Bourbon, in Moulins
Portrait of a Young Princess (Margaret of Austria, 1480-1530)
Tempera on panel; 13½″ × 9½″.
On the basis of the fleur-de-lys pendant with jewel (royal arms of France) the painting is dated 1490-1491, when the princess was betrothed to Charles VIII of France, a marriage which was annulled in 1491.
Robert Lehman Collection, 1975.

treatment up to 1946 when it was discovered in London and was acquired by Robert Lehman at auction. Despite this, it is a splendid picture, one of the finest examples of Fouquet's art. It is of particular interest for its documentary value. The view of the Île de la Cité, lapped by the curve of the Seine, Pont Saint-Michel leading to the imposing mass of Notre Dame on the left, the surrounding wall with its round towers, the bishop's palace, the bell-tower of Saint Michel, the towers of the Palais and the three large towers of the Petit Châtelet provide the most exact and detailed picture we have of Paris in the mid-fifteenth century. But Fouquet, while faithfully chronicling his city and its monuments, boldly added hills in the background to balance the heavy group of the Île with its roofs and trees, dominated by the massive bulk of Notre Dame. He also included in the gospel story the little black devils shown escaping out of the sides of the picture. The scene is viewed from high up on the Hôtel de Nesle where the group of praying figures is kneeling. This device—the representation of cities and landscapes from a high, distant viewpoint—dates back to Jan van Eyck and is frequently found in Flemish and later French painting. In many cities visitors were allowed up to high vantage points of this kind.

MASTER OF MOULINS. *Portrait of a Young Princess (Margaret of Austria).* p. 95

Previously thought to be a likeness of Suzanne, daughter of Pierre II de Bourbon and Anne de France, this work is now believed to be a portrait of Margaret of Austria, daughter of Emperor Maximilian I who became ruler of the Low Countries and a great patron of the arts. If this is so, as seems probable, the portrait must have been painted in about 1490 as Margaret was born in 1480 and is here shown as a young girl.

The portrait is undoubtedly by the same hand as the *Triptych* in the Moulins cathedral, the work which has given the artist his name. However, so far there is no biographical or artistic evidence to link the works of this master with any known artist. Attempts to identify him with Jean Perréal and the Flemish artist Jean Hay are unconvincing. In 1490–95 this French artist—or French by choice (there are works by him at Moulins and Autun)—still showed the influence of Hugo van der Goes and also had affinities with Fouquet. His work has a solemn, frequently monumental quality that can be seen even in his penetrating portraits.

GEORGES DE LA TOUR. *The Fortune Teller.* p. 97

In this superb "genre" painting La Tour combines two themes, that of the gypsy fortune teller popular in sixteenth century Italy, and the parable of the Prodigal Son, which was a favorite in sixteenth century France. Doubts about the picture's authenticity have now been shown to be without foundation. Various dates have been advanced, but the only fact of which we are certain is that La Tour was living in Lunéville, as his signature asserts, between 1620 and

GEORGES DE LA TOUR
Vic 1593—Lunéville 1652
The Fortune Teller
Oil on canvas; 40⅛″ × 48⅝″.
Signed (upper right): *G. de La Tour Fecit Luneuilla Lothar.* Possibly the artist's earliest known work, ca. 1620.
60.30
Rogers Fund, 1960

1636. An eighteenth-century provincial account tells us that La Tour was a pupil of Guido Reni, suggesting a decisive formative period in Italy possibly between 1610 and 1616. He was doubtless also aware of the works of Caravaggio, which contributed in a substantial way to Reni's early style. The composition is unified by a brilliant beam of light that creates a vivid contrast between the background and the figures in the foreground.

JEAN SIMÉON CHARDIN.   *Boy Blowing Bubbles.*   *p. 98*
Chardin's technical mastery was perfected during his long and rigorous apprenticeship with masters such as Coypel and van Loo, and he was also influenced by Dutch still-life and genre painting. The delicate tonalities and refined compositional style he assimilated in Paris from the work of the early eighteenth-century French artists harmonize successfully in the pleasing domestic and anecdotal scenes that form the main body of his work until 1771. Like Liotard, Chardin stands apart from his contemporaries, because he decisively rejected sixteenth- and seventeenth-century artistic formalism.

The version of the *Boy Blowing Bubbles* in the Metropolitan Museum is one of the earliest of the various paintings Chardin did of this theme. Another version, now unaccounted for, was exhibited in the 1739 Salon in Paris, and there are others in Washington, Kansas City and in private collections. This painting

JEAN BAPTISTE SIMEON CHARDIN
Paris 1699—Paris 1779
Boy Blowing Bubbles
Oil on canvas; 24″ × 24⅞″.
Signed (on stone at left): J. Chardin. Before
World War II successively in the collections of
D. David-Weill, Paris, and Fritz Ingres P. Am-
sterdam; then confiscated by the Nazis and sent
to the Führer Museum, Linz.
49.24
Wentworth Fund, 1949

suggests the impermanence and futility of human existence (and possibly also female inconstancy) and made a pair, at least in the 1779 sale of the Trouard collection, with the *Boy Playing Cards* that is now in the Oskar Reinhart Collection in Wintherthur.

JEAN ANTOINE WATTEAU. *Mezzetin.*

The painting shows Mezzetin, the valet and sentimental lover, a stock character of eighteenth-century Italian theatre. Scholars have often tried to identify the sitter for this picture. It is not Angelo Constantini, who first played the part of Mezzetin in 1683, nor is it Luigi Riccoboni, director of the Italian troupe that visited Paris in 1716. However we do know that Watteau kept Commedia dell'Arte costumes in his studio and liked his friends and models to dress up so

JEAN-ANTOINE WATTEAU
Valenciennes 1684—Nogent-sur-Marne 1721
Mezzetin
Oil on canvas; 21¾″ × 17″.
34.138
Munsey Fund, 1934

that he could paint them. The model for this picture may be the art dealer Sirois, a friend of Watteau's, who sat for the artist on other occasions.

The woodland background, with its delicate hues, provides a theatrical backdrop for the figure of Mezzetin, fully lit and vibrant with color. The light, pearly color indicates that the painting is a rather late work, as comparisons with the *Fêtes champêtres* of the Wallace Collection or the famous *Embarcation for Cythera* will confirm. It is generally agreed that it dates from about 1719. Its subsequent history is of interest. The painting was acquired by Watteau's patron, Jean de Jullienne. When Jullienne's collection was sold after his death in 1767, it was bought for the imperial collections of Catherine the Great. The canvas, which was framed as an oval, remained in Leningrad until 1931.

JEAN-AUGUSTE-DOMINIQUE INGRES
Montauban 1780 — Paris 1867
Madame Jacques Louis Leblanc (Françoise Poncelle, 1788-1839)
Oil on canvas; 47″ × 36½″.
Signed and dated (lower left, on the molding): flor 1823.
The picture was bought by Edgar Degas from the estate of Mme. Leblanc in 1896, and it remained in his collection until his death.
19.77.2
Wolfe Fund, 1918. The Catharine Lorillard Wolfe Collection

JEAN BAPTISTE CAMILLE COROT
Paris 1796 — Paris 1875
Reverie
Panel; 19⅝″ × 14⅜″.
Signed (lower left): COROT.
Formerly in the Hadengue-Sandras Collection, Paris, where it was known as "*L'Italienne.*"
29.100.563
Bequest of Mrs. H. O. Havemeyer, 1929
The H. O. Havemeyer Collection

JEAN-AUGUSTE-DOMINIQUE INGRES. *Madame Leblanc.* *p. 100, left*
In 1823, when Françoise Poncelle was thirty-five years old, Ingres painted this portrait and a portrait of her husband, Jacques Louis Leblanc. The Leblancs were then living in Florence, and were in the service of Elisa, Grand Duchess of Tuscany. After the two paintings had passed out of the sitter's family, they were acquired by Degas, who considered them the most prized items in his collection. On his death they were bought by the Metropolitan Museum. The large number of preliminary sketches that have survived bear witness to the extraordinary amount of thought that the artist put into the preparation of this portrait. The portraits may show the influence of Bronzino, and perhaps also of the early paintings of Caravaggio that Ingres had seen in the Giustiniani Collection in Rome. In the portrait of Madame Leblanc a cashmere shawl is draped sinuously over the side of the chair like a large striped cat, while the subject herself looks straight into our eyes, her skin as white as milk, her veiled body like that of a Persian odalisque.

JEAN-BAPTISTE-CAMILLE COROT. *Reverie.* *p. 100, right*
Between 1860 and 1870, Corot turned his attention to the single figure as a diversion from landscape painting. This is one of the most striking examples—the young woman is dressed in an "oriental" costume and arranged in a pose of poetic melancholy. The figure is actually constructed from volumes and planes skillfully matched to the scale of the blocks of stone in the background. The softly painted countryside and monochrome wall give exceptional prominence to the simple shapes revealed by the light falling on the figure. All this has, with good reason, reminded many people of other, similar but earlier, figures—the unforgettable creations of Jan Vermeer.

FERDINAND VICTOR EUGÈNE
DELACROIX
Charenton-Saint-Maurice 1798—Paris 1863
The Rape of Rebecca
Oil on canvas; 39½″ × 32¼″.
Signed and dated (lower right): Eug. Delacroix/1846.
Baudelaire praised the tones of this painting when it was exhibited in the Salon of 1846.
03.30
Wolfe Fund, 1903. The Catharine Lorillard Wolfe Collection

EUGÈNE DELACROIX.   *The Rape of Rebecca.*
Inspired by an unhappy episode in Walter Scott's famous novel *Ivanhoe,* the painter brings out all the exoticism, the passionate vehemence, and the violence of the drama. The whirling dynamism of the forms is accentuated by the stormy, smoky glare of the atmosphere.

The artist turned to *Ivanhoe* for subjects a number of times between 1829 and 1860. He made two versions of the *Rape of Rebecca,* a less emphatic, descriptive one in 1859, now in the Louvre; and thirteen years earlier this picture of 1846, executed when he was at the height of his maturity as a painter, and his inspiration by the work of his great master Rubens was more obvious.

AUGUSTE PRÉAULT.   *The Actor Rouvière Playing the Part of Hamlet and His Father's Ghost.*
Dated 1866, this relief originally bore Auguste Préault's signature, but later Dalou's signature was forged over it. Philibert Rouvière was another Frédéric Lemaître, an actor who was greatly appreciated by Flaubert. In the Goncourt *Journals* he is mentioned as an actor who borrowed gestures from works of art: "Rouvière uses despairing, epileptic gestures that remind you of Delacroix's lithographs of Faust." This remark also helps to explain Préault's bas-relief. He was still scarcely known when it was executed, but between 1830 and 1850

AUGUSTE AUGUSTIN PRÉAULT
Paris 1810—Paris 1879
The Actor Rouvière in the Role of Hamlet recoiling before the Ghost
Bronze, brown patina; 20½" × 24¼".
Founder's mark (lower left corner): F. Barbedienne, Fondeur (inscribed in model, heightened in finishing); dated 1866 (lower right corner inscribed in model, heightened in finishing). Inscribed (lower right corner), Dalou.
An apparently identical bronze relief signed "A. Préault" was used on the funerary monument of Rouvière at the cemetery of Montmarte. The inscription referring to Dalou on the Museum's example is spurious.
1972.2
Rogers Fund, 1972

he came to combine a disturbing romanticism with a realism similar to that of David d'Angers, for example in his statuettes (often in Sèvres porcelains) of figures or caricatures, that so appealed to Daumier, who himself made a series of painted busts.

JACQUES-LOUIS DAVID
Paris 1748—Brussels 1825
Antoine-Laurent Lavoisier and His Wife
Oil on canvas; 102¼" × 75⅝".
Signed and dated (lower left):
L. David (faciebat)/parisiis anno/1788.
1977.10
Purchase, Mr. and Mrs. Charles Wrightsman
Gift, 1977.

JACQUES-LOUIS DAVID. *Antoine-Laurent Lavoisier and His Wife.*
This portrait of Antoine-Laurent Lavoisier (1743–1794) and his wife, Marie-Anne-Pierrette Paulze (1758–1836), one of David's greatest works, was recently acquired for the Metropolitan. A key work in the development of eighteenth-century portraiture, it joins an equally famous interpretation of an antique theme, the *Death of Socrates*, painted in the preceding year.

Lavoisier, a celebrated statesman and chemist, is best known for his pioneering studies of oxygen, gunpowder, and the chemical composition of water. In 1789 he published the *Traité élémentaire de chimie*, an exposition of his theories, which was illustrated by his wife, who is believed to have been a pupil of David. Despite his service to the revolutionary regime, Lavoisier, a Farmer-General or tax collector, was arrested by order of the National Convention and, in 1794, sentenced to the guillotine. The portrait remained with his descendants for generations.

EDGAR DEGAS. *A Woman with Chrysanthemums.*

In nineteenth century one rarely finds pictures in which the human figure is given the secondary role, while the greater part is reserved for still-life. The idea of a prominently displayed vase of flowers and an off-center figure was used earlier by Courbet—in a painting of 1863 now in the Toledo Museum of Art—and again, somewhat later, by Millet. These painters shared an admiration for seventeenth-century Flemish still-life painting. Degas's picture may be one of the earliest works in which he resorted to photographs to give the effect of a fleeting pose. The presence of the two signatures and dates, 1858 or 1868 and 1865, has never been satisfactorily explained, nor has the subject been securely identified.

HILAIRE GERMAIN EDGAR DEGAS
Paris 1834 —Paris 1917
A Woman with Chrysanthemums
Oil on canvas; 29″ × 36½″.
Signed and dated: (twice, lower left)
Degas/18[5]8, and 1865/Degas.
Bought from the artist by Theo van Gogh for
Goupil & Cie., Paris.
29.100.128
Bequest of Mrs. H. O. Havemeyer, 1929
The H. O. Havemeyer Collection

MANET. *Boating.*

The Museum's outstanding collection of the works of Edouard Manet ranges from paintings of Spanish subjects, for example the famous *Spanish Singer,* to juvenile studies after Delacroix (*The Bark of Dante*) and Carracci (*Fishing in Saint-Ouen*), and to the portraits and still-lifes on which the artist concentrated in his last years.

Particularly happy, and representative of his most important period, when he was associated with Renoir and Monet, is this double portrait. The man may be his brother-in-law, Rodolphe Leenhoff; the identity of the woman is unknown. It was painted, together with the picture called *Argenteuil* in the Tournai Museum, during the summer of 1874, but unlike the latter, on which he worked for a long time, this canvas is said to have been completed in a very short time. So we are told by the painter Mary Cassatt, who persuaded the collector Mrs. Havemeyer to acquire it immediately, when they saw it on exhibition at the Salon. The speed at which it was painted gives the picture the freshness and spontaneity of a sketch.

EDOUARD MANET
Paris 1832—Paris 1883
Boating (1874)
Oil on canvas; 38¼″ × 51¼″.
Signed (lower right): Manet.
Exhibited at the Salon of 1879.
29.100.115
Bequest of Mrs. H. O. Havemeyer, 1929
The H. O. Havemeyer Collection

CLAUDE MONET. *Terrace at Sainte-Adresse.*

This early example of Monet's work—the picture was painted in the autumn of 1866—has recently been added to the impressive collection of his work in the Metropolitan Museum of Art. Other pictures of about the same date are a beach scene at Sainte-Adresse, painted during the following summer, and the well-known view of *La Grenouillère* of 1869. Monet's predominantly open-air scenes give an intense, momentary impression inspired by the artist's visual and emotional experience of his subject, but his compositions are based on a series of checks and balances and chromatic contrasts. The *Terrace at Sainte-Adresse* is one of the best examples of Monet's technique, with its bold orchestration of horizontals, verticals and diagonals. A strong light illuminates this precise counterpoint; range and touch are suggested by shading and the essential purity of color is brought out by its very transparency.

CLAUDE MONET
Paris 1840—Giverny 1926
Terrace at Sainte-Adresse (1866)
Oil on canvas; 35⅝″ × 51⅛″.
Signed (lower right): Claude Monet.
The first owner of this canvas was Victor Frat, Montpellier (a friend of Bazille), who bought it from the artist in 1868. Later for many years the painting was in the collection of the Rev. and Mrs. Theodore Pitcairn, Bryn Athyn, Pennsylvania.
67.241
Purchased with special contributions and purchase funds given or bequeathed by friends of the Museum, 1967

CÉZANNE. *Mont Sainte-Victoire.*

Mont Sainte-Victoire was one of Cézanne's favorite subjects, which he painted again and again from 1885 to 1887. Here the mountain itself is not so much the central theme, but forms an undulating background to the landscape. Cézanne painted the countryside from his brother-in-law Maxime Conil's house on the hill at Bellevue, with the viaduct stretching along the valley of the Arc in the distance. There is another version (whereabouts at present unknown) painted from a lower level with greater foreshortening of the middle ground.

A large wind-bent pine tree, often appearing in Cézanne's paintings, forms the axis: thrusting obliquely into the air, it divides the scene in two parts. The composition, bisected by the distant viaduct and by the diagonal line of the road, is carefully balanced, and the landscape is bathed in the sunny light of Provence.

PAUL CÉZANNE
Aix-en-Provence 1839—Aix-en-Provence 1906
Mont Sainte-Victoire (ca. 1885-87)
Oil on canvas; 25¾″ × 32⅛″.
29.100.64
Bequest of Mrs. H. O. Havemeyer, 1929
The H. O. Havemeyer Collection

CÉZANNE. *Madame Cézanne.*   *p. 108*

The Metropolitan Museum of Art possesses several major works by Paul Cézanne, from the early *Uncle Dominic* (1865–66) to *The Gulf of Marseilles* (1883–85), *Madame Cézanne in a Red Dress* (c. 1890) and the famous *Card-Players* (c. 1892). This portrait of *Madame Cézanne* was probably painted in

PAUL CÉZANNE
Aix-en-Provence 1839—Aix-en-Provence 1906
Madame Cézanne (ca. 1890-91)
Oil on canvas; 36¼" × 28¾".
61.101.2
Bequest of Stephen C. Clark, 1960

PIERRE-AUGUSTE RENOIR
Limoges 1841— Cagnes 1919
Young Girl Bathing (1892)
Oil on canvas; 32" × 25½".
Signed and dated, lower left corner.
The first owner of this painting was Claude
Monet, who had it in his collection at Giverny.
Robert Lehman Collection, 1975

1883–84 and is one of the finest examples of his work at the moment of his artistic maturity.

The brush strokes retain their initial freshness, the color its organic nature and the image is endowed with calm and serenity. It is unfinished only in the technical sense, for it is a vivid portrait, suggesting the essential qualities of the model, the painter's wife, Hortense Fiquet.

PIERRE AUGUSTE RENOIR. *Young Girl Bathing.*

After his so-called "severe" period, when Renoir, inspired by Raphael and the Florentines attempted to develop form in closely defined countours, he returned in the early 1890s to the pure painting of Impressionism. Yet in this vir-

PIERRE-AUGUSTE RENOIR
Limoges 1841 —Cagnes 1919
Madame Charpentier and Children (1878)
Oil on canvas; 60½″ × 74⅞″.
Signed and dated (lower right): Renoir. 78.
The painting was accepted for the Salon of
1879, and because of the influence of Mme.
Charpentier, was hung in a favorable position
and was important in establishing Renoir's rep-
utation.
07.122
Wolfe Fund, 1907. The Catharine Lorillard
Wolfe Collection

tuoso *Young Girl Bathing*, from the year 1892, the solidity of the figure nevertheless marks his increasing preoccupation with form, although now no longer
expressed in sinous outlines, but in terms of color values. This painting and
other similar nudes of young girls bathing he painted that year and the next
probably exemplifies Renoir's method as he described it to Walter Pach in
1908: "I arrange my subject as I want it then I go ahead and paint it, like a child
I want a red to be sonorous, to sound like a bell; if it doesn't turn out that way, I
put more reds or other colors till I get it . . . I look at a nude: there are myr-
iads of tiny tints. I must find the ones that will make the flesh on my canvas live
and quiver.''

RENOIR.   *Madame Charpentier and Children.*
Renoir's meeting with the family of Georges Charpentier, the publisher,
brought him new and valuable contacts with the established, highly cultivated 109

Parisian society of the day. The great portrait of Marguerite and her fair-haired children is an unforgettable record of a taste, a civilization and a way of life (Proust was to mention this picture fifty years later in *Le Temps Retrouvé*). It was exhibited in the Salon of 1879, acclaimed by public and critics alike, and firmly established the painter's reputation. In this work, a turning-point in his career, he aligned the four figures in a way that appears unstable but actually is structurally firm; after a hint of a pyramidal composition suggested by the areas of deep, vivid black in the clothes and the dog's coat, the composition is resolved into a diagonal alignment the upper part of which, with the writing desk and chair, is completed in the background. The lightness and spontaneity of the short "impressionist" brush strokes, the bright colors used to describe the two

110

HENRI ROUSSEAU (LE DOUANIER)
Laval 1844 —Paris 1910
Repast of the Lion
Oil on canvas; 44¾" × 63".
Signed (lower right): Henri Rousseau. Dated 1907 by Dora Vallier and cited as inaugurating the complex spatial arrangements of the later exotic landscapes.
51.112.5
Bequest of Samuel A. Lewisohn, 1951

IA ORANA MARIA

PAUL GAUGUIN
Paris 1848—Atuana, Marquesas Islands, 1903
Ia Orana Maria (1891)
Oil on canvas; 44¾″ × 34½″.
Inscribed (lower left): IA ORANA MARIA.
Signed and dated (lower right): P. Gauguin, 91
Gauguin wrote to his friend, de Monfreid, that
Ia Orana Maria, or *Hail Mary,* was the first
work of importance, as distinct from sketches
and studies, that he executed after his arrival in
Tahiti.
51.112.2
Bequest of Samuel A. Lewisohn, 1951

pretty children, the elegance of the surroundings in the "oriental" drawing-
room, the graceful furniture and the valuable ornaments, all add to the sense of
happy prosperity that emanates from this masterpiece of Renoir's maturity.

HENRI ROUSSEAU. *Repast of the Lion.* p. 110
Of all the pictures of animals, ranging freely or in conflict, of magical dreams or
transfigured biblical and allegorical scenes, that the Douanier set in the mysteri-
ous yet firm and flowery greenery of the jungle, this *Lion* is one of his most solid, best constructed works. The rhythm of the palm fronds—which in pictures

of this kind almost always create a sort of stage space in the extreme fore-ground—is here divided exactly in the middle like two opposite stage curtains, and behind, even the trees and the shrubs are aligned in an unusual pattern of verticals. The tawny beast and his prey, an almost immobile element, are anchored to the ground like plants amid the foliage of this fabulous forest. This painting is usually dated in the first decade of the twentieth century.

GAUGUIN. *Ia Orana Maria.*   *p. 111*
This was the first important picture that Gauguin painted in Tahiti, just after his arrival in what he hoped was to become his final refuge in an "innocent world" (1891). The firm discipline of the composition, the pure colors within the clearly outlined areas give form to a scene deliberately simple but full of interesting decorative elements, based actually on diverse sources, notably from Egypt and India, from Japanese prints and Peruvian art.

The sacred subject of the Annunciation, dressed up with exuberant Tahitian flora and peopled with impenetrable Maoris, was often used by Gauguin as a subject, in a watercolor, a charcoal drawing, and in engravings and monotypes. The figure of the woman appears alone in paintings entitled *Te Faruri, Parau Parau, Haere Pape.* It has been rightly pointed out that the source for the two figures praying in front of a flowering tree was a bas-relief in the temple of Boro-Budur which the artist knew from a photograph. This work is of fundamental importance in his artistic development, and was indeed regarded as such by Gauguin himself; he wanted to offer it to the Luxembourg Museum, but the director, Léonce Bénédite, refused it.

HENRI MATISSE. *L'Espagnole; harmonie en bleu.*
This signed work was completed by Matisse in 1923 at the Atelier des Ponchettes in Nice, according to the information given in the catalogue of the exhibition organized by Georges Petit in 1931. Despite its small size, the painting is one of the artist's most "musical" works: he has used his colors like a composer uses notes, and has created a series of chromatic variations, in which different rhythmical cadences are combined to produce a work of deceptively simple harmony. The result is a painting that demands almost total sensory involvement by the onlooker.

HENRI MATISSE
Le Cateau 1869 —Nice 1954
L'Espagnole; harmonie en bleu
Oil on canvas; 18½" × 14"
Signed (lower right), Henri Matisse.
Formerly in the collection of Gaston Bernheim de Villers, Paris.
Robert Lehman Collection, 1975

GERMANY

ALBRECHT DÜRER. *The Virgin and Child with St. Anne.*

Signed with the artist's monogram in the bottom right-hand corner, this is a splendid example of Dürer's painting in the years 1516–1520. This *Virgin and Child* was in the collection of the Electors of Bavaria at Schleissheim. In the Albertina in Vienna there is a drawing by Dürer for the "St. Anne," dated 1519, in which some scholars have recognized the features of his wife Agnes. This work is representative of the period in which Dürer was intentionally trying to rid himself of the artistic influences that he had absorbed during his first and second visits to Italy, and when, in attempting to preserve the compositional integrity his art (about which he developed many theories in his tracts on painting and geometry), he reverted to a much more Germanic type of characterization.

ALBRECHT DÜRER
Nuremberg 1471—Nuremberg 1528
The Virgin and Child with St. Anne (1519)
Tempera and oil on canvas, transferred from wood; 23⅝" × 19⅝".
Signed with monogram and dated (on background at right), 1519/A.D.
Previous owners include Gabriel Tucher, Nuremberg (until 1628); Maximilian I, Elector of Bavaria; the Royal Picture Galleries, Castle of Lustheim, near Schleissheim.
14.40.633
Bequest of Benjamin Altman, 1913

MOSAN ART. *Aristotle and Phyllis.*

A strikingly bold composition, this aquamanile representing Aristotle and Phyllis is an exceptional piece of secular sculpture from the beginning of the fifteenth century.

The story of Aristotle and Phyllis is a well-known medieval tale. While Alexander the Great was conquering Asia, he became so infatuated with Phyllis, an Indian girl whom he had taken as a wife, that he totally neglected the affairs of state. The alarmed dignitaries of the court sent his former tutor, Aristotle, the great philosopher, to plead for his return to his duties. The philosopher apparently did so to such purpose that the king turned his mind once more to the

MOSAN ART
Ca. 1400
Aristotle and Phyllis
Aquamanile, cast bronze; h. 13 3/16" × l. 15⅜".
Robert Lehman Collection, 1975.

business of state. Naturally, this did not please the queen, who, having found that Aristotle was at the bottom of her husband's coolness, resolved to revenge herself. She made advances to him, and in no time the old goateed philosopher was in love. As he was pressing her to requite his love, she said he must prove it by allowing her to ride upon his back. Aristotle, blinded by love, consented. Phyllis, in the meantime, had tipped off her husband so that he might observe the performance. It took place in a secluded garden where, after placing a saddle on Aristotle's back and a bit in his mouth, Phyllis rode upon him, the old philosopher crawling upon all fours. After witnessing the scene Alexander summoned Aristotle and demanded that he explain how his conduct could be so contrary to his advice. Whereupon the philosopher replied, "If a woman can make such a fool of a man of my age and wisdom, how much more dangerous must she be for younger ones? I added an example to my precept, it is your privilege to benefit by both." This fable is not of classical but of Indian origin, and had appeared in Islamic literature by the ninth century. It is impossible to tell how it reached the West; the Crusaders may have brought it back in the twelfth century. It was used by clerics to discredit the popular Aristotelian philosophy; lay scholars were greatly amused by the frivolous details. Hundreds of representations attest to the popularity of the tale in medieval art; the religious ones emphasizing the moral aspect, the secular ones the comic side.

The cunning damsel, attired in a modish dress with scalloped sleeves and a deep decolletage, triumphantly sits on the back of the philosopher and firmly grasps a tuft of his hair. His face expresses humiliation tinged with delight. The large hands and stretched limbs not only emphasize his ridiculous position, but firmly support the whole sculptural composition. The sculptural qualities are also outstanding: there are no superfluous details of drapery or decoration. Parts of the bodies are defined by large, uninterrupted volumes, such as the joined conical shapes of the upper torso and the thigh of the girl, the cylindrical limbs of Aristotle, and the unbroken, massive form of the sleeves. The ornamental decoration is sparing and never interferes with the main sculptural ideas of the composition; dotted circles mark the edges of her dress and the rosettes of his belt.

Who was the artist and in what circle did he work? The aquamanile bears no signature nor any other kind of mark. The dress of the two figures loosely dates it to the beginning of the fifteenth century. There is only one similar piece among the several hundred aquamanilia existing today, but that one (in the Musée Dobrée, Nantes) is, like ours, without signature or mark. Fortunately, the material and sculptural style of our aquamanile offer some help. The light yellow bronze points toward the famous bronze-working cities in the southeastern Netherlands, centered on the town of Dinant on the river Meuse. In the ateliers of these cities large-scale bronzes such as lecterns, candelabra, and baptismal fonts were produced in great variety during the fourteenth and fifteenth centuries. Some of these so-called *dinanderie* objects are well dated, and they are also stylistically related to the Burgundian sculpture of the time, especially to sculptures commissioned by the Burgundian dukes (in whose realm were these Mosan bronze-working cities). Several of the dated dinanderie works and Burgundian sculptures possess the refined sculptural qualities as well as the jocose secular spirit of our aquamanile, and therefore it seems appropriate to attribute it to a Flemish master working in the Mosan region around 1400.

116

LUCAS CRANACH THE ELDER
Kronach 1472—Weimar 1553
The Judgment of Paris
Tempera and oil on wood; 40⅛" × 28".
Painted ca. 1528.
28.221
Rogers Fund, 1928

LUCAS CRANACH THE ELDER. *The Judgment of Paris.* *p. 117*
Cranach was a prolific artist, and both he and his vast studio produced several versions of this scene from Greek mythology, but this particular one is unusual in that it shows a contemporary interpretation of a Classical theme.

In addition to being Burgomeister of Wittenberg, architectural adviser to the Elector of Saxony, bookseller and alchemist, the artist was also a friend of Martin Luther and one of the most important figures in the Reformation movement. His work often shows strong secular and Humanistic elements, and he made frequent use of mythological subjects, which, although superficially moralizing, barely conceal a strong sensual element. This is particularly true in the case of one of his favorite subjects, the clothed or unclothed female form.

LUCAS CRANACH THE ELDER. *Nymph of the Spring.*
Most of Cranach's life was spent in Wittenberg as court painter to three successive Elector-Princes of Saxony. He reflected the ideas of the German Reformation in intense religious paintings and in penetrating portraits of its leaders, Martin Luther and Philip Melanchthon. He also absorbed the artistic ideas of the Italian Renaissance in the humanist atmosphere of the court; this is apparent in the portraits of the dukes and their families and most of all in his innumerable paintings of mythological subjects.

The miniature-like *Nymph of the Spring* is signed (on the tree trunk above the head of the nude) with a winged serpent, a mark adopted by Cranach and his workshop after 1509. In the upper right-hand corner the inscription FONTIS NYMPHA SACRI SOMNVM NE RVMPE QUIESCO may be translated as "I am the nymph of the sacred spring, do not disturb my sleep, I am resting." According to Otto Kurz, this is an abbreviation of a pseudo-classical poem composed in the late fifteenth century. It was rumored among humanists of the time that the poem was on a statue of a sleeping nymph found in a grotto along the Danube. The poem inspired many representations of the nymph on Italian fountains, and she also appears in a drawing by Albrecht Dürer. Cranach probably used as his source paintings or engravings by Venetian artists, most likely those of Giorgione, and created a very popular composition. It was repeated by him and by his workshop many times; the earliest version is dated 1518, and judging by the style this one may have been painted as late as 1540.

The success of the painting lies in Cranach's skillful mixture of classical myth and Christian morality. The recumbent nude, clad only in her jewelry and in revealing veils, is the embodiment of temptation, surrounded by symbols of Venus such as the rabbits and the partridges in the lush vegetation. But her placement in a remote grotto, from which the spring issues, and the bow and quiver hanging above her head, are attributes of Diana, the virgin goddess of the hunt. Thus the classical subject has been transformed into a warning against the temptations of sensual desire.

HANS HOLBEIN THE YOUNGER.
Portrait of a Member of the Wedigh Family. *p. 120*
The subject, a man of twenty-nine years, has been tentatively identified as Hermann Wedigh, a merchant at the Steelyard in London and later town councilor

LUCAS CRANACH THE ELDER
Kronach 1472—Weimar 1553
Nymph of the Spring
Oil on panel; 6″ × 8″.
Robert Lehman Collection, 1975

at Cologne. Barthel Bruyn may have seen the painting in Cologne, for he seems to have copied the lower part in a portrait now in the Museum at Brunswick. At the time he painted this portrait Holbein was working the canvases—now lost (though known from drawings and engravings of a later date)—of the *Triumph of Wealth* and *Triumph of Poverty* for the Guildhall of the Steelyard merchants.

Holbein gives this portrait, and others that he executed at the beginning of his stay in London a distinctly Italian, Raphaelesque feeling. The face is turned three quarters towards the viewer, and the arm is placed so as to give the body, against a solid colored background, the static repose of a pyramid. The balustrade, a motif from Italian Quattrocento painting, was much favored by Holbein. The expression of the sitter is one of firmness and severity.

HANS HOLBEIN THE YOUNGER
Augsburg 1497—London 1543
Portrait of a Member of the Wedigh Family.
Tempera and oil on wood; 16⅝″ × 12¾″.
Signed and dated, with inscription: (center) ANNO. 1532. AETATIS. SVAE. 29; (on cover of book) H.H.; (on side of book) HER[ ]WID; (on paper in book) Veritas odiu[m] parit ("Truth breeds hatred," Terence *Andria*, line 69).
50.135.4
Bequest of Edward S. Harkness, 1940

FLANDERS
NETHERLANDS

JAN VAN EYCK. *Crucifixion and Last Judgment*, diptych.
In 1920 Durrieu identified these paintings, which are now attributed by most scholars to Jan van Eyck, as the doors of a diptych mentioned in the posthumous inventory of Jean, Duc de Berry. It has also been suggested that they flanked a representation of the Adoration of the Magi (which was stolen from a private collection in the nineteenth century). They are similar to the *Turin-Milan Hours*—compare the group of holy women in the *Crucifixion* with the *Pietà* in the *Turin Hours*—and show the early style of this great master of fifteenth-century Flemish art.

Van Eyck's inferno may have influenced Bosch. His *Last Judgment* was copied by Petrus Christus on the wing of a diptych dated 1452 that was originally in Spain and is now in the Berlin-Dahlem Museum. Van Eyck's interpretation of the biblical theme is traditional, but the exceptional freshness and accuracy with which he represented the natural world was revolutionary in its time.

JAN VAN EYCK
Maaseik ca. 1390—Bruges 1441
Crucifixion and Last Judgment (ca. 1425-1430)
Two panels, tempera and oil on canvas, transferred from wood; each 22¼" x 7¾".
These panels were originally parts of a triptych, the central panel of which, probably an *Adoration of the Magi*, was stolen when the triptych was in the possession of Prince D.P.Tatistcheff, Vienna and St. Petersburg. These panels subsequently were in the Hermitage (until 1933). The triptych was originally in a Spanish convent.
33.92 a, b
Fletcher Fund, 1933

ROGIER VAN DER WEYDEN. *Christ Appearing to His Mother.* p. 124
This panel, together with the *Nativity* and *Pietà* in Granada Cathedral, once formed a triptych. The paintings were bequeathed to the Cathedral by Queen Isabella of Spain, who died in 1504, and the two that remained there were subsequently cut down, but the original appearance of the triptych can be reconstructed from a nearly contemporary copy now in Berlin-Dahlem. The *Nativity* is set in an interior and the *Pietà* in a landscape, while in the Metropolitan Museum panel an elaborate Gothic edifice opens upon a luminous spring garden, where the Resurrection is depicted. A richly carved Gothic arch with tracery, colonettes and reliefs frames each composition. This is the work of Rogier's mature style, painted before 1445. While he owed much to van Eyck, as well as to the Gothic tradition, Rogier's intensely pathetic image is all his own.

PETRUS CHRISTUS. *Portrait of a Carthusian.* p. 125
A false frame painted by the artist is signed and dated at the bottom: PETRVS. XPI. ME. FECIT. A° 1446. The portrait is thus one of the earliest works of Petrus Christus, whose activity is documented from 1442, when he completed some paintings left unfinished by Jan van Eyck at the time of his death. The portrait is one of the original and suggestive works of this highly unconventional artist. The features of the bearded monk are sharply defined, but in addition, the artist concentrated on the clearest possible definition of cubic volume: the

ROGIER VAN DER WEYDEN
Tournai 1399—Brussels 1464
Christ Appearing to His Mother
Tempera and oil on wood; 25″ x 15″.
Inscribed on scroll held by the angel
at top; "*Mulier h[a]ec pleveravit
vi[n]cens o[mn]ia ideo data e[s]t ei
corona: ex apoc. vi-i* (This woman
fulfilled all things triumphantly;
therefore a crown was given unto
her. From the Apocalypse, VI,1). On
the border of the Virgin's cloak: the
words of the Magnificat.
This panel was originally the right
wing of a triptych, the other parts of
which are in the cathedral of Granada.
22.60.58

Bequest of Michael Dreicer, 1921

head within its conical scapular, and the pyramidal form of the shoulders, swathed in a white cloak. The frame, embossed like the cover of an antiphonary, and the minutely detailed fly on the lower edge, contrast in their fine detail with the voluminous structure of the head and shoulders. The intense light that illuminates the portrait is typically Eyckian.

PETRUS CHRISTUS
Active in Bruges 1444 — 1473
Portrait of a Carthusian (1446)
Tempera and oil on wood; 11½" x 8".
Signed and dated (below): PETRVS. XPI. ME.
FECIT. A° 1446.
It has been observed that this is the earliest
known formal portrait of a monk.
49.7.19
The Jules S. Bache Collection, 1949

PETRUS CHRISTUS. *St. Eligius.*   *p. 127*

In this unusually large fifteenth-century Flemish painting, the three almost life-size figures dominate the picture, in which a goldsmith sits at his counter in the open-street window of his shop, holding scales and a gold ring, while at his side stands a young couple in the bloom of youth, dressed in sumptuous wedding clothes. The subject has been traditionally identified as St. Eligius, Bishop of Noyon (the patron saint of goldsmiths) and St. Godeberta, whom the Bishop affianced to Christ in the presence of King Clothaire II of France. But the official form of this legend does not agree with the representation in this painting, which depicts the saint simply as an ordinary goldsmith (whose halo might have been a later pious addition)—not a bishop, but a craftsman selling a wedding ring to a noble couple.

According to tradition, the painting was commissioned from Petrus Christus by a goldsmith's guild, perhaps that of Antwerp, and in fact it was owned by the Guild of Antwerp until the middle of the nineteenth century. Because of the more than thirty detailed depictions of jewels and other precious objects, this painting is one of the most important sources of our knowledge of fifteenth-century goldsmith's work.

PETRUS CHRISTUS
Active in Bruges 1444—1473
St. Eligius (1449)
Oil on panel; 39" x 33 7/16".
Signed and dated below, on the edge of the workbench, *m petrus xpi me fecit a° 1449* (Master Petrus Christus made me in the year 1449), followed by the artist's emblem, which resembles a clock escapement over the outline of a heart.
Robert Lehman Collection, 1975

HANS MEMLING. *Portrait of a Young Man.*   *p. 128, left*

This fascinating portrait was at one time believed to represent St. Sebastian, as indicated by a halo around his head and an arrow in his hands, which were added at a later date—both have recently been removed in the course of meticulous restoration. One of Memling's finest male portraits, neither the identity of the sitter nor the date of the painting are known. The features suggest that he could have been a member of the large Italian colony in Bruges. Max J. Friedländer suggested a date for the painting between 1470 and 1475, which seems to be in accord with the style or the artist's dated paintings from this period. It is also the period when Memling produced some of the finest works of his extremely prolific career.

Undoubtedly an independent work rather than part of an altarpiece, the figure is not shown as a suppliant. The hands are calmly folded in repose and the figure carefully poised along the lines of a Florentine portrait, which in turn reflect the crystalline transparency of Flemish painting.

HUGO VAN DER GOES. *Portrait of a Man Praying.*   *p. 128, right*

The donor of an unknown altarpiece is shown with his hands joined in prayer in this fragment, probably from the left wing of a diptych, which would have been combined with an image of the Virgin and Child. It has been cut to an oval and the background was at one time painted over. The picture was once attributed to Antonello da Messina but more recent research has shown it to be the work of the Flemish master, Hugo van der Goes. It was painted late in his career, at the same time as the Portinari triptych in Florence, and is certainly among the finest of Flemish portraits.

HIERONYMOUS BOSCH. *Adoration of the Magi.*   *p. 129*

Very little is known about the chronology of the work of Hieronymous Bosch, but this must be one of his earliest paintings, as it is reminiscent of Geertgen tot Sint Jans and the Master of the Virgo inter Virgines. It seems most unlikely that, as has been suggested, the picture should be seen as an ingenuous attempt by Bosch's workshop to return to his early style at the end of his career. The figures are set in a severe, cell-like space, but the landscape is brightly illuminated, and in the background figures join a courtly procession, peasants dance and cows feed. Bosch has treated the solemn story of the Adoration in a light-hearted vein.

PIETER BRUEGEL THE ELDER. *The Harvesters.*   *pp. 130–131*

This grandiose scene is one of a series—of which five paintings have survived—representing the months of the year. The others are the *Hunters in the Snow,* the *Gloomy Day,* and the *Return of the Herd* in Vienna, and the *Haymakers,* now in Prague. Bruegel dated four of them 1565. The series may have been

Left
HANS MEMLING
Selingenstadt 1440—Bruges 1494
Portrait of a Young Man
Oil on panel; 15¼″ x 11⅛″.
A date between 1470 and 1475 has been suggested by Max J. Friedlander. Previously in the collection of Prince Anthony Radziwill, Berlin.
Robert Lehman Collection, 1975.

Below
HUGO VAN DER GOES
Ghent ca. 1440—In 1467 he became a Master at Ghent, where he worked until 1475; subsequently he was in the monastery of Roode Klooster, near Brussels, until his death in 1482.
Portrait of a Man
Tempera and oil on wood; 12½″ x 10½″.
Painted before 1475.
29.100.15
Bequest of Mrs. H.O. Havemeyer, 1929.
H.O. Havemeyer Collection

commissioned by the collector Niclaes Jonghelinck, for they are included in his collection as early as February 1566, and they were eventually acquired by the Archduke Leopold William.

In each one the men working and the landscape have a different rhythm, different colors and a different atmosphere evoke the seasons, yet they still form a coherent group, and convey a profound sense of nature. In *The Harvesters*, Bruegel's broad and fruitful landscape shimmers in the heat of midsummer. This large panel is dominated by the tree at the right, and the composition is organized around it. The eye is drawn upward, to the crown of overhanging branches, as well as downward, to the peasants resting in the foreground. Bruegel was to use the same device perhaps to even better effect, in the Munich painting of 1567.

HIERONYMUS BOSCH
's-Hertogenbosch ca. 1450 —active by 1480 —'s Hertogenbosch 1516
Adoration of the Magi (ca. 1490)
Tempera and oil on wood; 28″ x 22¼″.
13.26
John Stewart Kennedy Fund, 1912

Pp. 130–131

PIETER BRUEGEL THE ELDER
Bruegel (?) ca. 1525—Brussels 1569
The Harvesters
Oil on wood; 46½″ x 63¼″.
Signed and dated (lower right):
BRVEGEL /(MD)LXV.
19.164
Rogers Fund, 1919

PETER PAUL RUBENS. *Venus and Adonis.*

This *Venus and Adonis* by Rubens shows the influence of Italian art and of Titian, and it might well be compared with Titian's treatment of the same subject in the Prado. The figures are shown against a landscape typical of Rubens in his final years, and similar to the landscape in the *Andromeda in Chains* in Berlin. The countryside gleams in the autumn sunset, full of glimmering lights and reflections: not without reason has Rubens' later work been compared with that of Claude Lorrain.

Venus and Cupid hinder Adonis as he is about to set off for the hunt: the sensual, arcadian myth is here transformed by the Olympian genius of the aging Rubens—the painting can be dated about 1638—into a vibrant, luminous celebration of human existence. The model was his wife, Hélène Fourment, so often shown in his later works, each of which is more vital and original than the last.

PETER PAUL RUBENS
Sieghen 1577—Antwerp 1640
Venus and Adonis
Oil on canvas; 77½" x 94⅝".
Given by Joseph I, Emperor of Austria, to John Churchill, First Duke of Marlborough. The picture remained in the collection of the Dukes of Marlborough until sold by the Eighth Duke in 1886.
37.162
Gift of Harry Payne Bingham, 1937

ANTHONY VAN DYCK
Antwerp 1599—London 1641
Portrait of James Stuart, Duke of Richmond
and Fourth Duke of Lennox
Oil on canvas; 85" x 50¼".
89.15.16
Gift of Henry G. Marquand, 1889

FRANS HALS
Antwerp ca. 1580—Haarlem 1666
Young Man and Woman in an Inn
(*"Jonker Ramp and His Sweetheart"*)
Oil on canvas; 41½" x 31⅛".
Signed and dated (over fireplace, right):
F. HALS 1623.
14.40.602
Bequest of Benjamin Altman, 1913

ANTHONY VAN DYCK. *Portrait of James Stuart.*
Van Dyck went to live at the court of Charles I in 1635 and painted many portraits of the Duke of Richmond (1612–1655), a cousin and protégé of the King. This portrait of the Duke as a dashing young man in splendid attire was painted at the beginning of van Dyck's stay in London. Van Dyck concentrated on simple, uncluttered compositions: here the Duke and his greyhound are shown in a strong light that is both absorbed by the black satin costume and reflected off the trim of silver gilt and white lace. The shadowy background forms a subtle counterpoint.

FRANS HALS. *Young Man and Woman in an Inn.*
The couple are merrily drinking, but Hals gives only a glimpse of the tavern and the servant, filling the canvas with the figures and the curtain. This is certainly

HENDRICK TERBRUGGHEN
Deventer 1588—Utrecht 1629
The Crucifixion.
Oil on canvas; 61″ x 40¼″.
Signed and dated (lower center, on cross): *HT fecit 162-.*
56.228
Funds from various donors

an authentic work and some believe that it may actually represent Hals' version of the *Prodigal Son*. As in many other examples of Hals's work the artist shows a lively preference for unconventional subject matter, in an effect so as to free himself from the traditional discipline of more elaborate compositions. The diagonal arrangement stresses the couple in the foreground and creates a sharp recession into depth. In this shimmering painting the painter contrasts areas of thickly applied paint with patches executed with a minimum of brushstrokes. All the devices in this painting are employed to emphasize the joy of the scene.

HENDRICK TERBRUGGHEN. *The Crucifixion.* *p. 134*

Terbrugghen spent much of his early career in Italy (1604–1614), and the influence of Caravaggio, as well as of other artists, is apparent in this profoundly concentrated and intense *Crucifixion.* Although the choice and treatment of some details recall the work of Mantegna and Dürer, it is Grünewald, with whose works Terbrugghen was quite familiar, that served as the primary source. This can be seen for example, in the harshness of Christ's agonized contorsions, in Mary's undulating drapery as well as in her stunned expression, and in Saint John's painfully clasped hands.

All these influences and impressions blend marvellously to form a whole where all is subordinate to the impact of the tragic event. The brightness of the evening sky and the positioning of the lateral figures towards the foreground accentuate the artist's breadth of vision, and the scene gains an even greater immediacy as our eyes are drawn slowly upwards toward the figure of Christ. The resulting realism and simplicity makes the dramatic event seem only more supernatural.

REMBRANDT. *Portrait of Gérard de Lairesse.*

The painter and engraver, Gerard de Lairesse (1641–1711), was twenty-four

REMBRANDT VAN RIJN
Leyden 1606 —Amsterdam 1669
Portrait of Gérard de Lairesse
Oil on canvas; 44¼″ x 34½″.
Signed and dated (lower left): *Rembrandt fecit 1665.*
Robert Lehman Collection, 1975.

years old and a recent arrival in Amsterdam from Liège when Rembrandt portrayed him in this, one of the most powerfully evocative works of his final years (it is signed and dated "Rembrandt fecit 1665"). The tormented face of the young man, ravaged by syphilis, seems to have affected Rembrandt deeply at a time when he himself was passing through the bitterest years of a life beset with difficulties: it is as though the young man's suffering, with which the artist himself may well have identified, had provided him with the inspiration to show how man's inner strength could conquer evil and overcome the menace of death. The portrait illustrates Rembrandt's artistic technique very well: his images emerge slowly from the surrounding gloom, as if from some primeval chaos, gradually revealing themselves in the intermittent shafts of golden light that pick out the various details and bring the whole image to life.

REMBRANDT. *Portrait of a young man holding a book.*
It has been suggested that the subject of this portrait, signed and dated 1658, is the auctioneer, Thomas Jacobsz Haring, the man who conducted the enforced

REMBRANDT VAN RIJN
Leyden 1606—Amsterdam 1669
Portrait of a Young Man Holding a Book
Oil on canvas; 42¾" x 34".
Signed (on book): Rembrandt, F. 1658.
14.40.624
Bequest of Benjamin Altman, 1913

REMBRANDT VAN RIJN
Leyden 1606—Amsterdam 1669
Aristotle with a Bust of Homer (1653)
Oil on canvas; 56½" x 53¾".
Signed and dated (on pedestal of bust): Rembrandt f./ 1653.
The painting was commissioned by Don Antonio Ruffo, Principe della Scaletta, Messina, Sicily (1654-1673), and remained in the Ruffo family for over a century.
61.198
Purchased with special funds and gifts of friends of the Museum, 1961

auction of Rembrandt's possessions at the famous De Keysers Kroon tavern (the building still stands to this day). Everything that the painter owned—his house and all its contents, including his paintings, drawings, engravings, and his personal art collection—were all sold at ridiculously low prices.

Even though the shadowy outline of a bust on the table in the half-light of the background could perhaps be thought to lend credence to this theory, the almost reverential care with which the young man is handling the book is hardly typical of the brisk, business-like way in which an auctioneer runs through an inventory that he is hoping to sell as speedily as possible. His surroundings and his clothes are bathed in a gentle, yet very clear light, which, combined with the artist's subtle use of color, brings the scene into even greater relief, while the monumental verticality of the painting is further emphasized by the dramatic lighting on the hand in the lower part of the canvas.

REMBRANDT. *Aristotle with the Bust of Homer.*   *p. 137*

Between 1652 and 1663 Rembrandt painted three pictures for the house of Antonio Ruffo in Messina. They could almost be described as a triptych dedicated to the genius of mankind: besides the *Aristotle*, signed and dated 1653, which caused the man who had commissioned it considerable dismay (he thought that it looked "unfinished"), Rembrandt also painted *Alexander the Great* and *Homer Instructing Two of his Followers,* the latter completed in 1663.

The fire that broke out in 1848 in the gallery of the Ruffo family home destroyed many pictures, amongst them the *Alexander the Great*, two copies of which are now in the Glasgow Art Gallery and the Gulbenkian Collection respectively, as well as damaging many others. All that remains of the *Homer*, for example, is a fragment showing the head and shoulders of the poet, now in the Mauritshuis in The Hague, while the *Aristotle*, which had already been sold in 1760, has been preserved in its original state, apart from a few small areas of damage and possibly some slight tearing along the edge. The artist had obviously already planned a series of paintings of these three great men, who symbolize Poetry, Philosophy, and Politics, when he started on his *Aristotle*: not only does the subject have his hand on a bust of the poet (we know that Rembrandt himself possessed a similar one), but he is also wearing a medallion of Alexander on his richly painted robes. This sumptuous Oriental costume is of the same type that Rembrandt used for his Biblical figures; despite the fact that he ran the risk of being accused of a lack of realism, he was unwilling to depict authentic Graeco-Roman robes (of whose existence he was well aware), preferring to show the shimmering, glowing, gold cloth of his imagination.

JACOB VAN RUISDAEL. *Wheatfields.*   *p. 139*

The *Wheatfields* by Jacob van Ruisdael, one of the outstanding Dutch landscape painters of the second half of the seventeenth century, shows his love of the land and sky of his native Holland, and he magnificently describes the countryside and atmospheric effects. As in many of his works, he has chosen not to depict a calm sky but one which brings to mind an approaching storm. Two-thirds of the canvas is devoted to these growing clouds and the effect of light and shadow upon them. Below, Ruisdael arranges his landscape to en-

JACOB ISAACKSZ VAN RUISDAEL
Haarlem 1628 —Haarlem 1682
Wheatfields
Oil on canvas; 39⅜″ x 51¼″.
Signed (lower right): J V Ruisdael.
14.40.623
Bequest of Benjamin Altman, 1913

courage the viewer to enter the space: the country path widens as it approaches the picture plane, and we follow the vanishing point into depth, observing the changing effects of the brilliant sunlight.

VERMEER. *Woman with a Jug.* p. 140
This is one of the most beautiful of Vermeer's renderings of light pouring through a window into an interior. These scenes often present one or two illumined figures that appear in various situations and moods.

Although there is much disagreement about the chronology of Vermeer's work, this painting is generally dated to the years between 1658 and 1663. The great charm of the painting is its unusual blend of blues and golden yellows with whites and misty greys, the recurrent shading that softens the folds and lines of the fabrics, as well as the quality of the light shown on smooth bare walls. The young woman's gesture indicates that the real theme of the painting is the sun suddenly streaming in as she opens the window, perhaps to water the plants outside.

JAN VERMEER
Delft 1632—Delft 1675
Woman with a Jug
Oil on canvas; 18″ x 16″.
89.15.21
Gift of Henry G. Marquand, 1889

JAN VERMEER
Delft 1632—Delft 1675
A Girl Asleep
Oil on canvas; 34½″ x 30⅛″.
Signed (on wall to left of girl's head): J. VMeer.
14.40.611
Bequest of Benjamin Altman, 1913

VERMEER. *A Girl Asleep.*

In the catalogue of a 1696 sale, this painting appears under the rather ingenuous title of "Drunken Girl Asleep at a Table," and, ever since then, scholars have offered varying interpretations of the subject. Some have seen the sleeping woman as a representation of unrequited love (this is suggested by the painting in the background, over the girl's head, which shows the leg of a Cupid and his mask on the ground), while others see it as a straightforward image of a young woman grown drowsy from the wine she has been sipping from the glass on the table in front of her.

One of Vermeer's earliest works, it has been dated about 1655 on the basis of its similarity to Nicolas Maes' *Idle Servant* of the same year. The painting conveys a feeling of complete relaxation and tranquillity, almost in the manner of a still life. In the foreground, the folds of the Turkish carpet lead the eye from the gleaming pitcher, the bowl of fruit and the figure of the sleeping girl, towards the brightly lit interior revealed by the open door.

141

VAN GOGH. *Portrait of the Artist.*
Van Gogh's numerous self-portraits, executed throughout his career, reveal the artist's constantly changing style. This self-portrait, painted just after van Gogh went to Paris in 1886, typifies the critical moment when he began to use a more extended chromatic range. The thick brush strokes in this portrait with red beard and yellow straw hat give the impression of a bright sun sending out centrifugal rays. This is in direct contrast to the artist's earlier dark and more somber style, which can be seen on the verso, as van Gogh re-used an earlier canvas. On the other face the artist had depicted a sober seated figure peeling potatoes, which dates from his early years at Neunen (1883–84).

VINCENT VAN GOGH
Groot Zundert 1853—Auvers-sur-Oise 1890
Portrait of the Artist
Oil on canvas; 16″ x 12½″.
The painting dates from the artist's Paris period, ca. 1886-87.
67.187.70a
Bequest of Miss Adelaide Milton de Groot (1876-1967), 1967

VINCENT VAN GOGH
Groot Zundert 1853—Auvers-sur-Oise 1890
L'Arlésienne
Oil on canvas; 36″ x 29″.
Painted in 1888.
51.112.3
Bequest of Samuel A. Lewisohn, 1951

VAN GOGH. *L'Arlésienne.*
According to van Gogh's letters to his brother Theo, this portrait was "slashed on in an hour," in November of 1888. The sitter is Madame Ginoux, wife of the owner of a café in Arles which was frequented by both van Gogh and Gauguin. In fact, both artists executed portraits of this woman. Van Gogh painted another version at the same time, but with gloves and an umbrella on the table. That version is elaborate and less impetuous, showing more careful meditation on the theme. Then, in the winter and spring of 1890, when van Gogh was confined at Saint-Rémy, he used Gauguin's drawing of Madame Ginoux as he had no models to sit for him. The drawing was the source for four additional portraits of this friend of the artist.

SPAIN

EL GRECO. *Portrait of Cardinal Don Ferdinando Niño de Guevara.* p. 145

Niño de Guevara was created Cardinal in 1596, Grand Inquisitor in 1599 and Archbishop in 1601; he died in 1609. This superb portrait was probably painted to mark his receiving the cardinal's hat. The sitter is viewed full-length against a background divided into two parts by a panelled door and a golden damask cloth of honor. As in some earlier state portraits, his chair is placed diagonally, and the irregular, inlaid marble floor recedes in an oblique direction. The vortex of the divisions and movements generated by this composition is the face: the sitter scrutinizes the viewer with reserved concentration. The hands, one at rest, the other taut, accentuate the duality of his character.

EL GRECO (DOMENIKOS THEOTOCOPOULOS)
Candia (Crete) 1541?—Toledo 1614
Portrait of Cardinal Don Fernando Nino de Guevara (1541-1609)
Oil on canvas; 67¼" x 42½".
Signed (on paper lower center, in Greek): "Domenicos Theotocopoulos made it."
Formerly in the Oñate Collection, Madrid, where the painting had always been, belonging to the ancestral family of the Cardinal.
29.100.5
Bequest of Mrs. H.O. Havemeyer, 1929
The H.O. Havemeyer Collection

EL GRECO. *St. Jerome as a Cardinal.* p. 146

In this late work of ca. 1604–05, St. Jerome is represented as an ascetic scholar and visionary lost in thought. Several identifications have been proposed for the subject: a member of the Venetian Cornaro family, or the archbishop of Toledo, Gaspar de Quiroga, in the guise of the saint. But there is now general agreement that the painting is an idealized representation of St. Jerome. Altogether there are five known versions of the composition, of which this and the one in the Frick Collection, New York, are considered the finest.

The sumptuous color of the cardinal's brilliant red robe against the greenish black background contrasts with the green tablecloth, the white sleeves and the open Scriptures. The painting is an interesting example of El Greco's use of "deforming mirrors" to elongate, dilate, contort, twist and foreshorten his subjects, giving them an amazing plasticity and sense of tension, such as this thin, spectral figure weighed down by his sumptuous robes.

EL GRECO. *View of Toledo.* p. 147, left

From 1577 until his death thirty-seven years later in 1614, El Greco spent a long period working in Toledo. During this time he concentrated a significant part of his activity painting views of the city itself. These were included in such representations as the *St. Martin* at Washington, the *St. James the Greater* in the Museum of Santa Cruz at Toledo, the *St. Joseph and Child* in the Chapel of San José in Toledo, and three versions of the Laocoön. The Metropolitan Museum's painting is one of two independent landscapes preserved. Less factual than the *Panorama with the Map of Toledo* (El Greco Museum, Toledo), which shows the roads and buildings as they really were in a calmer, sunlit ambience, it resembles the backgrounds of various religious pictures, where the features of the city have been re-arranged and the lighting is dramatic. This subjective attitude to landscape painting is responsible for the intensely poetic effect.

EL GRECO. *Vision of St. John.* *p. 147, right*

This extraordinary painting seems to have been inspired by St. John's description of the Opening of the Fifth Seal in the *Book of Revelations* (6:9-11)—"And when he (the Lamb) had opened the fifth seal, I saw under the altar the souls of those who were slain for the word of God . . . And white robes were given to every one of them." The painting has been considerably cut down at the top; the altar and Lamb of God mentioned in the text were presumably represented in this missing area. This is one of the three large altar paintings commissioned by the Hospital of St. John Outside-the-Walls in Toledo in 1608, but the artist evidently left it incomplete at his death in 1614. Of the other two, The *Baptism of Christ* is still in the Hospital, while the *Annunication* is now in the Banco Urquijo in Madrid. The latter picture is also missing a piece at the top, fortunately preserved in the National Gallery of Greece in Athens.

146

EL GRECO (DOMENIKOS
THEOTOCOPOULOS)
Candia, (Crete) 1541?—Toledo 1614
St. Jerome as a Cardinal
Oil on canvas; 42½" x 34¼".
Formerly in the collection of Marquis del Arco,
Madrid.
Robert Lehman Collection, 1975.

El Greco has interpreted this supremely visionary scene in a strikingly unnaturalistic fashion. The flame-like movement of the figures; the cool, acidic colors; the juxtaposition of the large figure of St. John and the diminutive ones of the Resurrected—without any indication of the space separating them—make an impression of tension and disembodiment appropriate to the apocalyptic subject matter.

VELASQUEZ. *The Supper at Emmaus.* *p. 148*

Most likely dating from an early moment in Velasquez' career, this painting is remarkable for the pictorial devices employed: the simple background against which the figures are silhouetted, the peasant character of the two pilgrims, the somber colors, and the focused light used to create vivid contrasts. These are elements of a new style of painting evolved by the Italian Caravaggio to create an immediate impact and give greater veracity to sacred stories. Velasquez has, moreover, placed Christ at the left of the composition instead of at its center, as was usually done. The result is a more dynamic design and a masterly contrast between the expressions of surprise and revelation of the pilgrims and the calm, shadowed countenance of Christ as he blesses the bread.

Another version of this scene, attributed to Velasquez, eventually found its way into the collection of King Louis Philippe of France, but the work in the Metropolitan is the original, on which the later painting was based.

Below

EL GRECO (DOMENIKOS THEOTOCOPOULOS)
Candia (Crete) 1541?—Toledo 1614
View of Toledo (ca. 1600-1614)
Oil on canvas; 47¾" x 42¾".
Signed (lower right, in Greek script): "Domenicos Theotocopoulos made it."
The painting belonged to the ancestral family of the cardinal, the Onate. It was purchased from them by Durand-Ruel and sold to H.O. Havemeyer in the early years of this century.
29.100.6
Bequest of Mrs. H.O. Havemeyer, 1929
The H.O. Havemeyer Collection

Right

EL GRECO (DOMENIKOS THEOTOCOPOULOS)
Candia (Crete) 1541?—Toledo 1614
The Vision of St. John (ca. 1610-14)
Oil on canvas; 88½" x 78½".
At one time in the collection of Ignacio Zuloaga.
56.48
Rogers Fund, 1956

VELASQUEZ. *Juan de Pareja.*

Velasquez painted this extremely fine portrait of his trusted assistant, the mulatto Juan de Pareja, in 1650, while he was in Rome acquiring works of art on behalf of the Spanish King. It has been suggested that it was done as a sort of trial run for the more imposing and official *Portrait of Pope Innocent X.* We know for a fact that it was put on display at the annual exhibition at the Pantheon, and that it excited universal admiration: one connoisseur is alleged to have exclaimed, "Everything else may be art, but this is Truth."

Though in this late portrait Velasquez still uses the strong illumination and light background typical of Caravaggio, his palette is limited to a dazzling sequence of greys and warm flesh tones. The composition is equally restrained. The imposing and proud figure is placed diagonally with the head almost frontal. The right arm crosses the torso to provide a firm base in a fashion reminiscent of some of Raphael's most famous portraits. This scene is enlivened by marvelously deft brush strokes.

FRANCISCO DE GOYA. *Bullfight.* *p. 150*

A late work, dating from about 1812, this painting is one of many landscapes and scenes of popular festivals which Goya executed in the years that followed the restoration of the Bourbon dynasty. During the nineteenth century it

DIEGO RODRIGUEZ DE SILVA Y VELASQUEZ
Seville 1599—Madrid 1660
Juan de Pareja (1650)
Oil on canvas; 32" x 27½".
After belonging to William Hamilton, Palazzo Sessa, Naples, the painting was long in the collection of the Earls of Radnor, Longford Castle, England.
1971.86
Fletcher Fund, Rogers Fund, Bequest of Miss Adelaide Milton de Groot (1876-1967), supplemented by gifts from the Friends of the Museum, 1971

DIEGO RODRIGUEZ DE SILVA Y VELASQUEZ
Seville 1599—Madrid 1660
The Supper at Emmaus (ca. 1620)
Oil on canvas; 48½" x 52¼".
14.40.631
Bequest of Benjamin Altman, 1913

formed part of the Salamanca Collection in Madrid, along with its companion picture *Procession at Valencia* (now in the Bührle Collection, Zurich).

Goya has depicted a double arena in which two bullfights are taking place. On the right is the moment of lancing when the bull is charging the picador, while on the left the matador is preparing his sword, inciting the bull with a red cloth. A volatile crowd watches from banks of seats and from makeshift platforms. The two scenes are viewed from above, a fence providing the visual link between the animation of the foreground and the teeming crowds that lie beyond, silhouetted against the warm light of the evening. The extremely loose brush work enhances the impression of immediacy and excitement.

A smaller version of this painting, formerly in the Academia de San Fernando, is now in the Prado.

FRANCISCO DE GOYA.   *Majas on Balcony.*   p. 151
Majas on a Balcony, together with its companion picture, *The Maja and Celes-*

FRANCISCO DE GOYA Y LUCIENTES
Fuendetodos 1746 —Bordeaux 1828
The Bullfight (ca. 1810-20)
Oil on canvas; 38¾" x 49¾".
Listed in the inventory of pictures in Goya's house when they were made over to his son Xavier, after his mother's death in 1812. Identified as one of "four equal paintings," the other three now dispersed in other museums.
22.181
Wolfe Fund, 1922. The Catharine Lorillard Wolfe Collection

FRANCISCO DE GOYA Y LUCIENTES
Fuendetodos 1746—Bordeaux 1828
Majas on a Balcony (ca. 1810)
Oil on canvas; 76¾″ x 49½″.
29.100.10
Bequest of Mrs. H.O. Havemeyer, 1929
H.O. Havemeyer Collection

tina, appears in the 1812 inventory of the artist's personal effects. Those two paintings are now in a Swiss private collection and the March Collection in Palma de Majorca, respectively, while the one in the Metropolitan is a signed version of the original, completed during the same period (probably in about 1805, and certainly not later than 1812). It is, if anything, an even more brilliant and expressive work. The modifications made by the artist, changes in emphasis rather than full-scale alterations, have succeeded in creating a tighter, more unified composition in which the contrast between the women and rather sinister men in the gloomy background is emphasized. The balcony is used to separate the figures from the viewer as well as relate pictorial and real space. The compelling effect obtained evidently pleased Manet, whose *Balcony* at Paris is based on one of Goya's paintings. There are two other near-contemporary versions of this scene in private collections.

PABLO PICASSO. *Portrait of Gertrude Stein.*

As far as can be gathered, the American expatriate writer (1874-1946) posed for this portrait more than eighty afternoons in the studio of Rue Ravignan during the winter of 1906. The following spring when the artist and the writer went their separate ways—Gertrude Stein to Italy and Picasso to the Pyrenees—the artist declared his dissatisfaction with the portrait and erased the face. Then on his return to Paris in the autumn he repainted it as it is now. Gertrude Stein wrote, ''It is the only portrait that is all me.'' In fact it seems Picasso attempted less a character study than research into form, inasmuch as the painting was so drastically changed and repainted. Following his first attempts at planar stratification, he has shown Gertrude Stein in a shallow setting within a clear architectonic structure using a pyramid shape reminiscent of Raphael and the Italian tradition. Without an x-ray examination it is hard to tell what alterations were made between the first and second versions of the head, but it now appears as a flat plane with details modelled in chiaroscuro, as in other works he painted in 1908 as part of his interest in Negro art and his first steps towards cubism.

PABLO PICASSO
Malaga 1881—Mougins 1973
Portrait of Gertrude Stein (1906)
Oil on canvas; 39⅜" x 32".
47.106
Bequest of Gertrude Stein, 1946

ENGLAND
UNITED STATES

ROBERT PEAKE THE ELDER. *Henry Frederick, Prince of Wales.*

The inscription around the sides of the painting identifies the two boys as Henry Frederick, Prince of Wales (1594-1612) and John Harrington (1592-1614). The date 1603, the year in which James VI of Scotland, the father of this young prince, was proclaimed King of England as James I, is engraved on the tree trunk, while two heraldic shields with the royal arms are suspended from branches. The young prince has just enacted the ritualistic climax to the hunt—the severing of the deer's head. Too young to fully accomplish this task, he sheathes his sword with great flare. Although the painting is the first of a type of portraiture given final form by van Dyck, it is as conspicuous for its del-

ROBERT PEAKE THE ELDER
Active in London 1576/8—1626
Henry Frederick, Prince of Wales (1594-1612)
and Sir John Harrington (1592-1614)
Oil on canvas; 79½" x 58".
Inscribed: (left) 1603 fe/AE 11/Sir John Harrington; (right) 1603/feAE 9/Henry Frederick Prince of Wales Son/of King James the lst.
44.27
Purchase, Joseph Pulitzer Bequest, 1944

THOMAS GAINSBOROUGH
Sudbury 1727—London 1788
Mrs. Grace Dalrymple Elliott
Oil on canvas; 92¼" x 60½".
Painted ca. 1778.
Previously belonging to the Cholmondeley family, Houghton Hall, King's Lynn, Norfolk.
20.155.1
Bequest of William K. Vanderbilt, 1920

icate execution and charm. In the past this work was attributed to the famed miniaturist, Isaac Oliver, but recent scholarship has revealed it to be the masterpiece of a less well-known contemporary, Robert Peake.

THOMAS GAINSBOROUGH. *Mrs. Grace Dalrymple Elliott.* *p. 155*
This portrait is a typical work of Gainsborough's last years in London, the culmination of this great portrait and landscape painter's career. His favorite motifs are found in this canvas, the gorgeous silks, the precious embroidery, the rosy flesh, the elaborate, delicate coiffure, the face of the young woman, portrayed in profile, at once thoughtful and alert. Only the short train of her dress connects the landscape with this sweet apparition, caught in a delicate balance of suspended motion. The effect of depth is emphasized, with an artifice not commonly found in Gainsborough, by the narrowness of the opening onto the outdoor background, with its threatening clouds, heavy foliage and unexpected gleams of light.

JOHN CONSTABLE
East Bergholt 1776—London 1837
Salisbury Cathedral from the Bishop's Garden
Oil on canvas; 34⅝" x 44".
50.145.8
Bequest of Mary Stillman Harkness, 1950

During a visit with the Bishop of Salisbury, John Fisher, in 1820, Constable made some sketches of the cathedral as seen from his grounds. By 1823 one of these had been turned into the painting now at the Victoria and Albert Museum, London. Exhibited at the Royal Academy with considerable success, it was destined for the Bishop's residence in London. During the following two years Fisher commissioned a smaller version as a gift for his daughter and what became another full-sized variant of the original, now in the Frick Collection. He had lamented the dark storm cloud in the first version, so Constable brightened the sky and parted the trees. The Metropolitan painting follows this scheme. The sky and grass have a silvery tonality and the sun beats full on the cathedral. To the left are the Bishop and his wife while a herd of Suffolk cows grazes in the shade. There is an airy lightness to the foliage of the trees which gives this version a special appeal. It is possible, however, that this quality is due to the fact that the painting is unfinished. If so, it may be the work mentioned in the Executors' sale of Constable's works as ''Salisbury Cathedral, from the Bishop's garden, *nearly finished.*''

JOSEPH MALLORD WILLIAM TURNER
London 1775 —London 1851
The Grand Canal, Venice (ca. 1835)
Oil on canvas; 36″ x 48⅛″.
99.31
Bequest of Cornelius Vanderbilt, 1899

TURNER. *The Grand Canal.* *p. 157*

In 1820 Turner spent two weeks in Venice sketching views and, above all, transcribing the magical light of the city into watercolors of great subtlety. It was not until 1833, however, that he exhibited the first two of a long line of Venetian subjects in his annual exhibits at the Academy. One of these was titled *Bridge of Sighs, Ducal Palace and Customhouse, Venice: Canaletto painting.* As the title suggests, it paid tribute to the great eighteenth-century painter of Venice. In 1835 he exhibited *Venice, from the Porch of the Madonna della Salute;* this is identical to the painting in the Metropolitan, which shows the steps leading up to the porch of S. Maria della Salute. A sketch for the composition is dated 1835. Not surprisingly, to the great critic, John Ruskin, the work appeared as a challenge to Canaletto. Despite the fact that Turner may have revisited Venice before 1835, his attention to the carefully diminishing buildings on the Grand Canal and the thinly clouded sky is indeed very much in the manner of the earlier master. The colors, however, are Turner's alone: the contrasting blues of the sky and water, the touches of red in the boats. He has also created a brighter, more luminous ambience by employing the palette knife to suggest effects of light.

EDWARD HICKS
Langhorne, Pa. 1780 —Newtown, Pa. 1849
Peaceable Kingdom (ca. 1830)
Oil on canvas; 18″ x 24″.
Inscribed (lower right center, in black):
ISAIAH 11 Chap 6 7 8.
1970.283.1
Gift of Edgar William and Bernice Chrysler
Garbisch, 1970

EDWARD HICKS. *Peaceable Kingdom.*

A Pennsylvania Quaker, Edward Hicks was a highly productive painter and one of the most vigorous and original of the American "primitives" or "natives"—artists without any academic or professional training.

In this canvas he celebrates a happy state of nature where no enmity exists between man and fierce wild animals. It is an entirely fideistic, inspired view of the Biblical Garden of Eden, an Utopia of earthly existence which corresponds perfectly with Hicks's style of painting. Apart from a few simple elements of ordered and related composition, he achieves all the eloquence of a sermon through the images and their direct appeal to the spectator that sets up a sort of dialogue between the artist's vision and the outer world.

GEORGE CALEB BINGHAM.

Fur Traders Descending the Missouri. *p. 160*

George Caleb Bingham is considered the main exponent of American genre painting. He was born in Virginia in 1811 and died in Missouri in 1879, and during his early career was a self-taught, completely spontaneous artist. Only in 1838 as an art student at the Pennsylvania Academy of Fine Arts and in New York did he become aware of the Hudson River School of landscape painting and the luminous works of Thomas Cole. During a student journey to Dussel-

ISAIAH 11 chap 6

dorf in 1856-59, Bingham found new ideas and fresh incentive in the Romantic work of contemporary and earlier nineteenth-century German painters.

Before 1856, Bingham's paintings and drawings have a frontier directness, but with none of the epic-heroic style of J. Fenimore Cooper—his irony is more akin to that of Mark Twain. *Fur Traders Descending the Missouri* is one of the outstanding masterpieces of nineteenth-century American art. Painted in 1845, it is very similar in mood to some of Thoreau's more contemplative written descriptions—there are points in common with the latter's *A Week on the Concord and Merrimac Rivers*—and also to Hawthorne. There is a rapturous sense of balance and peerless rhythm in the images reflected on the water, shown against the infinite horizon of mists beyond the river-banks, with the glimmer of sunshine lighting up the dust with all the marvelous luminosity and purity of classical art.

GEORGE CALEB BINGHAM
Virginia 1811—Kansas City 1879
Fur Traders Descending the Missouri (ca. 1845)
Oil on canvas; 29″ x 36½″.
One of four paintings purchased by the American Art Union late in 1845. The painting was originally titled "French Trader and Halfbreed Son." Two drawings in the Mercantile Library, St. Louis, are sketches for figures in this painting.
33.61
Morris K. Jesup Fund, 1933

160

HISTORY OF THE MUSEUM
AND THE BUILDING

American Paintings and Sculpture

The Museum's founding trustees included several American artists; an architect, a sculptor and four painters. The Museum bought little American art during its first 30 years, happily able to rely upon gifts and bequests. Many important paintings were thus acquired. Trumbull's *Alexander Hamilton* from Henry Gurdon Marquand in 1881, Gilbert Stuart's *George Washington* from H. O. Havemeyer in 1888, Charles Willson Peale's full-length *Washington* from Collis P. Huntington in 1896, and Matthew Pratt's *The American School* from Samuel P. Avery in 1897. The Museum started to buy contemporary American works of art after George A. Hearn gave funds in 1906 and 1911, as did Morris K. Jesup and Maria DeWitt Jesup in 1915. At times the Museum organized influential shows of St.-Gaudens, Homer, Ryder, Eakins and other artists. The most ambitious exhibition of contemporary American art was the *Artists for Victory* show in 1942, for which three regional juries selected almost 1500 paintings, sculptures and prints from all over the country. In 1949 a separate Department of American Art was established, and in 1970 a Department of 20th Century Art was established which assumed care for art created by artists born after 1875. The Museum's collection of American art is probably the most broadly representative that there is. In the newly enlarged American Wing it will be shown to the best advantage in the galleries, period rooms, and study storage.

The American Wing

In 1909 the Metropolitan celebrated Henry Hudson's exploration of the Hudson River in 1609 and Robert Fulton's start of steam navigation in 1809. The Museum's Hudson-Fulton Exhibition pioneered by showing Dutch paintings in America and by gathering American painting and house furnishing "to test out the question whether American art was worthy of a place in an art museum." This question by the Metropolitan's president, Robert W. De Forest, was answered by such popular enthusiasm that he was able to persuade Mrs. Russell Sage to give the museum a New England collection of 600 pieces of 17th- and 18th-century American furniture. De Forest and R. T. H. Halsey then worked together to assemble a series of American rooms from about 1670 to 1820, fitting them ingeniously together in chronological order behind the 1822 marble facade of the U. S. Branch Bank, which De Forest had moved from Wall Street. In 1924 the American Wing opened with an ovation that has made it the Metropolitan's most imitated feature and has strengthened interest in preserving historic buildings. In 1931 the Wing added the elaborate entrance hall of the Van Rensselaer House in Albany and in 1941 an 18th-century interior furnished with the belongings of the Verplanck family of New York. For the Museum's centenary in 1970 the Wing organized a revealing exhibition called *Nineteenth-Century America* that explored a new way of presentation to be used in an enlargement of the Wing which will bring its story up to Frank Lloyd Wright. In 1924, *A Handbook of the American Wing* by Charles Cornelius and R. T. H. Halsey provided the first reliable history of the applied arts in North America.

Ancient Near Eastern Art

The Ancient Near East Department of the Metropolitan Museum of Art was officially created in 1956 when all of the pre-Islamic art from the Middle East was gathered together under the curatorship of Charles K. Wilkinson. The collection of ancient objects, however, began long before that time. In 1932, John D. Rockefeller Jr. gave the colossal guardian figures and the Assyrian reliefs from the Northwest Palace of Ashur-nasirpal at Nimrud. Throughout the 1950's the Department participated with the British School of Archaeology in Iraq in the excavation of Nimrud and in exchange received many of the fine ivories that were found there. In the 1950's and 60's the museum purchased fine examples of Near Eastern art, including the two heads of rulers and the gazelle cup illustrated on pp. 25-27. In 1974 an agreement was made by which the Metropolitan Museum head of a statuette of Ur-Ningirsu, a neo-Sumerian ruler, was joined to its body in the collection of the Départment des Antiquités Orientales of the Musée du Louvre. Now the complete statuette is shown for alternating three year periods at each museum. The Department continues to participate actively in excavation in the Near East. One of the projects currently in progress is the excavation, in southern Iraq, of Al-Hiba, the capital of the city-state of ancient Lagash, which began in 1968 under the directorship of Vaughn E. Crawford, the present Curator-in-Charge of the Ancient Near-East Department.

Arms and Armor

As early as 1875 the Museum held a loan show of the Cogniat collection of armor, and in 1896 it accepted the gift of 166 pieces from Mrs. John Ellis. Historic treasures came in 1904 when Rutherford Stuyvesant secured the Parisian collection of the Duc de Dino. To catalogue this purchase the Museum borrowed the curator of fishes from the American Museum of Natural History, Bashford Dean, also an armor collector who had just lent his Japanese armor to the Metropolitan. Dean became the curator of arms and armor from 1912 until he was elected trustee in 1927. In 1913 he persuaded William H. Riggs to give the collection that he had intelligently and passionately assembled during 60 years of travel in Europe. Riggs asked that his donation be merged with the armor already in the Metropolitan "so that the Museum's exhibit of arms and armor should illustrate in an unbroken series all the stages of the armorer's art." His gift made this ideal possible. Dean designed a helmet and body armor for use in World War I, which was not adopted until World War II. In 1926 he excavated the Crusader castle of Montfort in Palestine. The second curator, Stephen Grancsay, secured remarkable pieces such as the Greenwich suit of the Duke of Cumberland. The present curator, Helmut Nickel, has organized many special exhibitions and has written an illuminating social history of his subject. The Metropolitan's armor collection spreads over more types and styles than can be found in any other single place, and it displays them in a dramatic historical sequence.

The Costume Institute

In 1937 Irene Lewisohn opened a Museum of Costume Art in a loft on West 46th Street to help designers in the nearby theatres. The collection moved to Rockefeller Center in 1939 when the war stopped Europe's fashion industry and threw American designers on their own. As soon as New York's dress designers discovered inspiration so close at hand, the Museum of Costume Art outgrew its small rooms. In 1946 it moved, as the Costume Institute, into the Metropolitan Museum where it could tap the resources of great historic collections. There in 1971 it opened quarters rebuilt to provide exhibition galleries, a library, private study rooms for designers, and safe storage for conserving 30,000 items of historic costume. The Costume Institute has led the way in inventing and perfecting techniques for restoring and preserving costumes, and in the dramatic staging of exhibitions that often forecast fashion trends. The needle trades—New York's most powerful industry—show their appreciation by supporting the Institute with proceeds from a gala party each year.

Drawings

The collection started in 1880 when Cornelius Vanderbilt gave 670 17th- and 18th-century Italian drawings that had been gathered in Florence by James Jackson Jarvis. Then in 1910 Mrs. George Blumenthal gave three Matisse drawings, the first of his to enter any museum. In 1929 the Havemeyer Collection brought in seven Rembrandts, two Daumier watercolors and 25 Baryes, all of the highest quality. Excellent Fauve and Cubist drawings were given in 1949 by Georgia O'Keefe from the Alfred Stieglitz Collection. The curators of paintings bought ten Degas drawings from the artist's estate auction in 1917, four Leonardos, including his pen study for the nativity, Michelangelo's red chalk study for the Libyan Sibyl in 1924, 50 Goyas from all periods of his life in 1937, the Biron collection of Venetian and French works of the 18th century in 1937, and Rubens' pen studies for the *Garden of Love* woodcuts in 1959. The collecting of drawings has become more active and systematic since a special department was established in 1960 under Jacob Bean. During his curatorship many drawings have been bought, including Raphael's red chalk study for the *Madonna in the Meadow* in Vienna. A distinguished series of drawings came in with the bequest of Walter C. Baker, and more fine ones from Harry G. Sperling, who also bequeathed a purchase fund, which served to acquire a sheet of studies for allegories by Veronese. The Lehman Collection, while not a part of the Drawings Department, has enriched the Museum with a superb series of drawings by many famous masters. The Department has organized important exhibitions, sometimes in collaboration with the Morgan Library.

Egyptian Art

In 1895, while Cesnola was director, the Museum subscribed to the Egypt Exploration Fund and received objects excavated by Flinders Petrie and others. In January 1907 Albert M. Lythgoe, who had been digging in Egypt with George A. Reisner, began to excavate for the Metropolitan at Lisht; he later went to the Kharga Oasis, and in 1910 opened a concession at Luxor, where digging continued until 1936. The excavation was first financed by J. P. Morgan, then extensively by Edward S. Harkness, with contributions from the Rogers Fund. In 1920 Lythgoe's pupil, Herbert Winlock, discovered the extraordinary models of Egyptian life from about 2,000 B. C. in the tomb of *Mekutra*. In addition to excavated objects, the Department also benefited from purchases and gifts. In 1913 Harkness bought the mastaba tomb of *Pernebi* at Saqqara and installed it in the Museum. In 1915 Theodore M. Davis bequeathed 1,100 Egyptian objects found during his personal excavations in Egypt; and in 1926 Harkness gave the finest private collection of Egyptian small and precious objects, gathered by Lord Carnarvon. In a number of purchases the Museum acquired some of the most exquisite jewelry that has survived antiquity, belonging to princesses of the Middle Kingdom, Hyksos Period, and XVIII Dynasty. Its most recent significant purchase was a blue faience sphinx with the cartouche of *Amenhotpe* III. In addition to these acquisitions, the Department received the sandstone Temple of Dendur, a gift of the Egyptian people to the people of the United States; a special wing has been built to house it. In 1976 the present Curator, Christine Lilyquist, opened the first segment of a reinstallation of the collection in the most instructive sequence of Egyptian art to be found anywhere.

European Paintings

A few months after the Museum was founded in 1870, it purchased 174 European paintings in Paris, which included Poussin's *Midas Bathing in the River Pactolus*. William T. Blodgett and the Museum's first president, John Taylor Johnston, backed the purchase and were repaid by subscription. In 1887 Catherine Lorillard Wolfe bequeathed 143 paintings, many of the Barbizon School, and provided a fund out of which the Museum later bought Goya's *Bullfight*, Delacroix's *Abduction of Rebecca*, Daumier's *Don Quixote* and Winslow Homer's *Gulf Stream*. In 1889 the second president, Henry Gurdon Marquand, gave 37 paintings that he had bought with extraordinary perspicacity especially for the Museum. These included Vermeer's *Woman with a Jug*, van Dyck's supremely elegant *Portrait of James Stuart*, three Hals portraits, and works by Petrus Christus, Ruysdael, and Gainsborough. Also in 1889 Erwin Davis gave Bastien Lepage's *Joan of Arc* and the first pair of Manets ever to enter a public collection—the *Boy with a Sword* and the *Woman with a Parrot*. The collection started to grow in earnest in 1904 when J. P. Morgan was elected president and the Rogers Fund became available. He engaged Roger Fry to purchase paintings for the Museum and for himself during five stormy years. Fry and his assistant, Bryson Burroughs, curator from 1909 to 1934, managed between them to have the trustees buy Renoir's *Mme. Charpentier and her Children* in 1907 (the first Renoir ever bought by a public collection) and in 1910 Veronese's *Mars and Venus United by Love*, Tintoretto's *Doge Alvise Mocenigo Presented to the Redeemer*, and Rubens' *Wolf and Fox Hunt*. The next year brought Giotto's *Epiphany*, Botticelli's *Three Miracles of St. Zenobius* and Carpaccio's *Meditation on the Passion*. Burrough's foresight and courage made the Metropolitan the first museum to buy a Cézanne in 1913. 1913 also brought the bequest of Benjamin Altman with Botticelli's *Last Communion of St. Jerome*, Titian's *Portrait of a Man*, Vermeer's *Girl Asleep*, four works by Memling and two by Velazquez. In 1916 J. Pierpont Morgan, Jr. gave Raphael's early *Madonna and Saints*, to which the Museum added one of its original

predella panels in 1932. In 1919 Burroughs purchased Brueghel's *Harvest* from his series of the months. The Havemeyer bequest in 1929 brought Hugo van der Goes' *Portrait of a Man*, Bronzino's *Portrait of a Young Man*, El Greco's *View of Toledo* and *Portrait of Cardinal Niño de Guevara*, Goya's *Majas on a Balcony*, and an incomparable wealth of Impressionist works by Courbet, Degas, Manet, Renoir, Cézanne and Cassatt. During the Depression of the 1930s the Museum managed to secure Mantegna's *Adoration of the Shepherds*, Watteau's *Mezzetin*, Titian's *Venus and the Lute Player*, and van Eyck's *Crucifixion* and *Last Judgment*, while Harry Payne Bingham gave Rubens' *Venus and Adonis*. In 1943 Maitland Griggs bequeathed Sassetta's *Journey of the Magi* with twelve other early Italian paintings shortly after Edward S. Harkness had left Lawrence's *Countess of Derby* and Pollaiuolo's *Portrait of a Young Lady*. Jules Bache's bequest of 63 paintings included Titian's *Venus and Adonis*, a Madonna by Crivelli, Rembrandt's *Standard Bearer*, Velazquez' *Infanta Maria Theresa*, Watteau's *French Comedians*, Fragonard's *Billet Doux*, and Goya's *Don Manuel Osorio*. Samuel A. Lewisohn's bequest in 1951 brought Gauguin's *Ia Orana Maria*, Seurat's sketch for *La Grande Jatte*, and van Gogh's *Arlésienne*. The Museum of Modern Art, in return for a subsidy in 1943, gave the Metropolitan "classic" works of the 19th and 20th century, including two Cézannes, three Matisses and Picasso's *Woman in White*, later joined by Picasso's *Portrait of Gertrude Stein*, willed to the Metropolitan by the writer in 1946. In 1967 Adelaide Milton de Groot bequeathed paintings of the School of Paris that she had lent to the Museum since 1938, including van Gogh's *Self Portrait* and Toulouse-Lautrec's *Englishman at the Moulin Rouge*. In 1969 the great and varied Robert Lehman Collection added its own galleries of early Italian panels, Botticelli's *Annunciation*, a Memling portrait, Rembrandt's *Portrait of Gérard de Lairesse*, El Greco's *St. Jerome as a Cardinal*, Ingres' *Portrait of the Princesse de Broglie*, and many more recent works. In the meantime, under the curatorship of Theodore Rousseau, the Museum bought Velazquez' *Count-Duke of Olivares on Horseback* and Caravaggio's *Musicians* in 1952, Georges de La Tour's *Fortune Teller* in 1960, Rembrandt's *Aristotle with a Bust of Homer* in 1961, and Velazquez' *Juan de Pareja* in 1971. The collection as a whole represents European painting in excellent—and often superlative—examples, with particular emphasis on the Netherlands and the Impressionists.

European Sculpture and Decorative Arts

The Department of Decorative Arts was founded in 1907 under W. R. Valentiner, absorbing the collection of an earlier Department of Sculpture and Casts. As this vast section grew, it spawned over the years the departments of Far Eastern Art, American Decorative Arts, Near Eastern Art, Medieval Art, and 20th Century Art. The original urgency to form a department for the decorative arts was occasioned by J. P. Morgan's gift in 1907 of 18th-century French porcelain, woodwork, furniture and textiles from the Hoentschel collection, in order "that it should be made the nucleus of a great collection of decorative arts." A decade later, J. Pierpont Morgan Jr's gift of hundreds of Renaissance and later objects, especially goldsmith's work and horology, greatly increased this position of importance.

In 1910, Thomas Fortune Ryan's gift of Rodin sculptures gave new thrust to the sculpture collections. The Benjamin Altman bequest (1914) brought fine sculptures of the Italian Renaissance as well as of the French 18th century. In the following decades, an occasional masterpiece such as Tullio Lombardo's *Adam* was acquired by purchase. Recently, the French sculpture holdings have been much enriched by gifts from two foundations headed by Col. C. Michael Paul.

The first of many stellar pieces of French royal furniture came in 1920 when William K. Vanderbilt bequeathed a black lacquer commode and secretary made by Riesener for Marie Antoinette. More superb royal furniture has been given lately by Mr. and Mrs. Charles Wrightsman to furnish sumptuous panelled rooms that they have installed as well as rooms previously given by Susan Dwight Bliss and Mrs. Herbert N. Straus. The Museum is in fact preeminent in its series of furnished period rooms. Exquisite French furniture inlaid with Sèvres plaques was given by the Samuel H. Kress Foundation, which also gave the room from Croome Court with its tapestries by Boucher on the walls and furniture. In 1932 the

Museum bought the neoclassical dining room from Lansdowne House, designed by Robert Adam, and in 1939, the intarsia panels made for Federigo da Montefeltro's study in the palace at Gubbio. Another Renaissance landmark is the marble patio from the Castle of Velez Blanco near Murcia from the large and varied bequest of George Blumenthal (1941). A later Spanish treasure is the great iron choir screen from Valladolid Cathedral, given in 1956 by the Hearst Foundation.

In 1948, the bequest of Catherine Wentworth brought magnificent French silver. Beginning in 1937, R. Thornton Wilson contributed to the ceramics collection until it now represents every major factory from the 15th through the 18th centuries. German porcelains and German rococo furniture of particular distinction were willed to the Museum in 1974 as the Leslie and Emma Sheafer Collection. The latest of many remarkable gifts and bequests is the collection of Judge Irwin Untermeyer, adding superlative objects to virtually every category in the Department and raising the representation of English silver and woodwork to the best outside England.

Far Eastern Art
This department has received many gifts because Americans were long ago attracted to Japan, then China, and recently to India and Southeast Asia. Already in 1879 some 1,300 Chinese porcelains were bought by subscription. A Han bronze was given in 1887 by the Chinese diplomat, Chang Yen Hoon, as the first of a splendid series that now covers the development from the early dynasties onwards, with masterpieces such as an altar set of 14 pieces and a rare and exquisite shrine dated AD 524. In 1902 Heber R. Bishop bequeathed over 1,000 jades of all sorts. The ceramic collection covers the production of 4,000 years, thanks to the generosity of J. P. Morgan, Benjamin Altman in 1913, Samuel T. Peters in 1926, and John D. Rockefeller, Jr. in 1960. Systematic purchasing began when Sigisbert Chrétien Bosch-Reitz became the new department's first curator from 1915 to 1928, after which Alan Priest took over until 1960. During these years when China allowed the export of works of art, the series of monumental Chinese sculptures grew into the most varied one to be found in any single place. There are also many sculptures from outside China, such as a large standing gilt bronze Buddha of the Gupta period and a Khmer bronze of a kneeling queen, recently purchased out of the Florance Waterbury Fund. The purchase of the Bahr Collection brought many Chinese paintings, and other purchases have added the Sung painting of *The Tribute Horse* in 1941, and the Han handscroll *The Shimmering Light of the Night* in 1977 from the Dillon Fund. Among the Japanese screens there is a wave by Korin and an iris garden by his school. The Far Eastern collection is to be reinstalled in galleries given by Dr. Arthur Sackler.

Greek and Roman Art
The classical collection was the first section of the Museum to draw international attention in 1874 and 1876 when General Luigi Palma di Cesnola sold the Metropolitan 6,000 objects that he had excavated on Cyprus. The island's then unfamiliar hybrid style made these perfectly genuine sculptures seem like fakes. When Cesnola became the Museum's first director until his death in 1904, he used the new Rogers Fund in 1903 to make three remarkable purchases: the first lot of ancient glass for what has now become the world's best collection; a hoard of Etruscan bronzes from near Spoleto, including a sculptured ceremonial chariot; and finally frescoes from near Naples, where the eruption of Vesuvius in AD 79 had preserved the only Roman painted room now outside Italy. When Edward Robinson, the first trained American archaeologist, transferred from the Museum of Fine Arts in Boston to the Metropolitan in 1904, later becoming director from 1910 to 1931, he instituted the systematic buying of classical art. The Museum began purchasing Greek sculptures in 1908 with the uncompromising Hellenistic marble of an old market woman; then the fifth century gravestone of a girl with two doves in 1927; the imposing archaic grave monument in various purchases; the archaic giant kouros in 1932; the bronze *Sleeping Eros* in 1943; the most sensitive version of the Aphrodite of the Medici type in 1952; the extremely elaborate Roman sarcophagus in 1955; and many fourth-century Attic gravestones. Consistent purchasing has amassed a continuous series of pottery from Minoan times to the end of the Roman Empire, with highlights like the group of huge archaic

grave urns and the calyx-krater painted by Euphronios. The galleries occupy two floors, with the heavy stones below and most of the lighter things above.

Islamic Art
The collection took shape in 1891 when Edward C. Moore bequeathed outstanding Persian and Hispano-Moresque pottery, Egyptian, Syrian and Mesopotamian metalwork and glass, including the largest series of enameled glass mosque lamps outside Cairo. These categories were greatly enriched by gifts from J. P. Morgan, Isaac D. Fletcher, George D. Pratt and the Havemeyer family. These donations, and the special gifts of Alexander Smith Cochran in 1913, and of N. M. Grinnell in 1920 assembled a wide coverage of Islamic miniature painting, now capped by Arthur A. Houghton, Jr.'s gift of 78 leaves from a sumptuous Shad-nameh illuminated in Tabriz by the best Persian painters of the early 1500s. The extraordinary collection of carpets came from the gifts of mainly Turkish work from James S. Ballard and of the finest carpets of all kinds from Joseph V. McMullan. The department's constant purchases have added the monumental brass incense burner shaped like a feline, cast in Persia in 1181, a brilliant faience mosaic prayer niche made in Isfahan in 1354, and two Hapsburg treasures—the enameled bottle illustrated on page 44 and the 16th century "Emperor" carpet abandoned by the Turkish general after the last siege of Vienna in 1683. From 1935 to 1940 the Museum's excavations at Nishapur, conducted by Joseph Upton, Walter Hauser and Charles K. Wilkinson, brought in carved and painted stucco wall decorations, and pottery of a type then almost unknown. Maurice Dimand, the department's first curator from 1932 to 1959, wrote *A Handbook of Muhammadan Art* (1944) which is the first such history in English, and was translated into Persian, Arabic and Urdu. In 1975 the present curator, Richard Ettinghausen, gathered the collection together out of store rooms and many parts of the museum to make a logical presentation in a spectacular series of galleries that reveal the department's unique spread through time and place in the whole Islamic world.

The Robert Lehman Collection
Robert Lehman's bequest in 1969 covers almost every aspect of European art since 1300. The series of paintings, starting with Italian gold-ground panels, features the largest Sienese group outside Siena, and continues with such Renaissance masterpieces as Botticelli's lyrical *Annunciation*. Northern painting is well represented with a splendid group of van Eyck's immediate followers, starring Petrus Christus' *St Eligius*, signed and dated 1449, and continuing through the 17th century with such masterpieces as Rembrandt's haunting portrait of Gérard de Lairesse. French painting is distinguished by a page from Fouquet's famous Book of Hours, and Ingres's aristocratic last portrait of the Princesse de Broglie, and a good showing of the early 20th century. Spain contributes two impressive El Grecos and Velazquez' fresh study of the Infanta Maria Teresa. The drawings form one of the most astonishing sections of the collection, ranging from an extraordinary number from the 15th century through works by many of the famous masters until after 1900. The Renaissance furniture from Italy and France is consistently of palace quality, while the Renaissance jewels and carved hardstones make a sumptuous display. The collection occupies a special pavilion like a museum within the museum, where some of the rooms from the Lehman family house have been reconstructed.

Medieval Art and the Cloisters
In 1907 J. P. Morgan, that collector of collections, lent the Museum his two great medieval collections, the Georges Hoentschel woodwork, ivories, Limoges and Mosan enamels on copper, and the matchless Svenigorodskoi collection of Byzantine enamels on gold, as well as six of the nine most sumptuous surviving late antique silver plates sculptured with the story of David, and possibly made for the Emperor Heraclius about 630. In 1917 J. Pierpont Morgan, Jr. gave his father's great loan—over 7,000 objects—establishing a sort of medieval museum at one blow. In 1921 Michael Dreicer's bequest added rare Romanesque stone figures, among them a writing prophet probably from Chartres Cathedral. George Blumenthal's bequest in 1941 brought an ivory plaque of the Emperor Otto II dedicating Magdeburg Cathedral about 970 and a monumental Mosan oak Madonna of about 1220. In 1945 Mrs. Harold Irving Pratt gave the early 15th-century Franco-

Flemish tapestry of the Annunciation. In general, however, the later effort in medieval art went into the Cloisters rather than into the collection on Fifth Avenue.

This branch museum originated in 1906 when George Gray Barnard, needing money to continue his sculpture in France, made it by dealing in medieval carved stones. Along with many statues, he bought Romanesque and Gothic cloister ruins from St.-Michel-de-Cuxa, Bonnefont-en-Comminges, St.-Guilhem-le-Desert and Trie. In 1913 he brought all his purchases to New York and assembled them near Fort Tryon. The next year John D. Rockefeller, Jr. purchased 56 acres around Fort Tryon to make a public park, for which he acquired, in 1925, Barnard's museum to rebuild it at the northern end of the hill over the city's grandest view of the Hudson. Fitting the architectural units together on the sloping terrain required long planning by the architect, Charles Collins with Mr. Rockefeller, Joseph Breck, then curator of Decorative Arts, and finally with James J. Rorimer. When the Cloisters finally opened in 1938 it already displayed Mr. Rockefeller's supreme gift, the Unicorn tapestries. With his generous endowment the Cloisters bought the Antioch Chalice, the 13th-century stone Virgin from the rood screen of Strasbourg Cathedral, the 12th-century frescoes from San Pedro de Arlanza, Roger Campin's Mérode triptych of the *Annunciation*, and the 12th-century ivory cross from Bury St Edmunds. The Cloisters is the only place outside Europe where the unique achievement of the Middle Ages—its architecture and architectural sculpture—can make its full appeal through a setting of intelligent simplicity.

Musical Instruments

The musical instruments collection began in 1884 with the gift of a Spanish church bell, and by 1889 the collection numbered some 45 instruments, most of them the gift of Joseph Drexel. In 1889 Mary Crosby Brown donated her assemblage of 276 instruments, many of them non-European, and over the next 18 years Mrs. Brown developed this nucleus into one of the world's largest comprehensive collections. Today the musical instruments department holds about 4000 objects. Among the most famous are a virginal made for the Duchess of Urbino in 1540; the oldest extant piano, made by its inventor Bartolommeo Cristofori in Florence in 1720; and the only Stradivari violin ever restored to its original condition. Under the supervision of Curt Sachs many instruments were restored to playing condition in the 1930s. Emanuel Winternitz, curator from 1942 to 1973, originated a concert series that attracted many people to the Museum and led to construction of the Grace Rainey Rogers Auditorium. In 1971 Mrs. Clara Mertens generously enabled the Museum to construct the André Mertens Galleries for Musical Instruments, in which a cross-section of both European and non-Western instruments is permanently displayed. The present department head, Laurence Libin, began in 1973 to expand activities in the areas of acquisition, restoration, performance, and cataloguing.

Primitive Art

The Metropolitan acquired its first objects of "primitive art"—a collection of Peruvian and Mexican antiquities—in the 1880-1890s. Some time later, on the assumption that it was archaeological and, even more, ethnological material, it was later placed on loan at the American Museum of Natural History and other museums.

Primitive art is now used as an expression designating the arts of Pre-Columbian America, Africa and Oceania. Valued since the early years of the 20th century by scholars and artists, the arts of these areas have been the object of growing public appreciation for their originality and subtlety. This was confirmed by René d'Harnoncourt's innovative exhibitions of American Indian, South Seas and ancient South American art from 1941 to 1954 at the Museum of Modern Art. Probably the greatest private collection to be formed in this period is that of Nelson A. Rockefeller, who later gave it to found the Museum of Primitive Art, which opened in 1956. The collection had a spectacular showing at the Metropolitan in 1969; at that time Rockefeller pledged the collection to the Metropolitan Museum on completion of a new Wing to be named in honor of his son, Michael C. Rockefeller. The Metropolitan Museum itself formed a Department of Primitive Art, to maintain its existing collections, including those given by Nathan Cummings and Mrs. Alice K. Bache.

The Michael C. Rockefeller Wing will be opened in Spring 1979; housing extensive galleries, a library, and a photographic archive, it will become an important center for studies and public display area in the field.

Prints and Photographs

This department started as the Department of Prints in 1916 when Harris Brisbane Dick bequeathed his print collection and a purchase fund. The first curator, William M. Ivins, Jr., a brilliant young lawyer without museum experience, laid down the policy that a museum print collection "must be, like the library of a professor of literature, composed of a corpus of prints in themselves distinctly works of art, filled out and illustrated by many prints which have only a historical technical importance." In 1919 Junius Spencer Morgan partly gave and partly sold the Dürer collection that he had perfected over many decades. Between the World Wars, Ivins bought Gothic and Renaissance woodcuts, brilliant impressions of Mantegna, Schongauer, ES and Goya as well as many Baroque and Mannerist prints. During his curatorship from 1916 to 1946 his arresting exhibitions and his incisive writing attracted remarkable gifts and bequests—Americana from James Allen Munn; Gothic woodcuts from James C. McGuire; Rembrandt, van Dyck and Mary Cassatt from the H. O. Havemeyer bequest; Rembrandt and Dürer from George Coe Graves; Gothic prints and late Rembrandts from Felix M. M. Warburg and his family; Currier & Ives from Alice S. Colgate; ephemeral prints from Bella C. Landauer and Jefferson Burdick. These gifts have made a Rembrandt collection that is smaller than that in the Morgan Library, but rich in superb impressions of his late etchings. Purchases have built up an extensive series of ornament, where the most famous item is the bulk of the drawings for Chippendale's *Cabinet Maker's Director*. Ivins, fascinated by the marriage of word and image, collected a large proportion of the great illustrated books from the blockbook to now. In 1928 Alfred Stieglitz gave the first photographs—his own works—and later followed this with the gift of a unique series of Pictorialist photographs that he had assembled for *Camera Work*. Through purchases, many made possible by David Hunter McAlpin, the collection acquired work by Fox Talbot, D. O. Hill and other early photographers. As a whole, the collection is smaller than those in Vienna, Paris and London, but covers a wider field than any of them.

Textile Collection

The Textile Study Room, the first of the study rooms at the Metropolitan was opened in 1909 in response to the same Victorian ideal as the Victoria and Albert Museum in London and the Cooper Union Museum for the Arts of Decoration in New York—to make fine examples of the decorative arts available for close study by any accredited person.

A plea in the Museum Bulletin in 1906 had resulted in the donation of fine lace collections, the result of the then fashionable hobby of lace-collection, by the society women of New York. To these were added the great collections of Mrs. Magdalena Nuttall and of the Blackthornes to form the nucleus of what has become one of the great lace collections of the world. The collection of historic textiles of Friedrich Fischbach purchased at the time of the opening of the study room was the first of many great acquisitions in that field. Miss Frances Morris, the first curator, became a world-famed expert. The Needle and Bobbin Club, founded by Miss Morris and fellow enthusiasts under the aegis of the Textile Study Room in 1916 has remained a close friend of the Museum ever since. Continuing important acquisitions—the purchase of Renaissance and Rococo silks and velvets from the Sangiorgi collection, the bequest of the great collection of Chinese textiles and costumes by William Christian Paul, John Jacob Astor's gift of his late wife's superb lace—have made the Museum's textile holdings outstanding.

Twentieth Century Art

In 1967 the Metropolitan director, Thomas P. F. Hoving, felt that the Museum should complete its encyclopedic range by inaugurating a special Department of Twentieth Century Art to gather together paintings, sculpture, drawings and the decorative arts from various departments, and to add to them as important works were created. For The Metropolitan's centenary in 1970 the curator of the new department, Henry Geldzahler, assembled over 400 works for an exhibition of *New York Paintings and Sculpture: 1940–1970*. Since then historic 20th-century objects and new trends in contemporary art have been constantly shown in a series of galleries assigned to the new department.

THE BUILDING

The dynamic growth of the Museum's collections, notably during the past forty years, is reflected in the history of the building. From the original Calvin Vaux Ruskinian Gothic structure initiated exactly a century ago, through Richard Morris Hunt's colossal Neoclassic plan for the extension of the building along Fifth Avenue and his Great Hall (1895), followed by McKim, Mead, and White's grandiose Fifth Avenue facade and large open courts, to subsequent structural additions, the successive plans of the Museum have never been able to keep pace with the demands for accommodating the continuing flood of acquisitions, nor the incredible growth of attendance and related activities.

To meet this demand, the Trustees in 1967 approved the formulation of a Master Architectural Plan for the Metropolitan's second century. The firm of Kevin Roche John Dinkeloo and Associates was given the commission to develop the Plan. Of the vast additions and alterations now under way under this plan, only the Fifth Avenue Entrance, the restoration of the Great Hall and the Lehman Pavilion have been completed. Some idea of what the Museum will look like when the Plan is realized can be gained from the architect's model reproduced here. The reproduction is keyed to some of the main areas of the new Museum in the making.

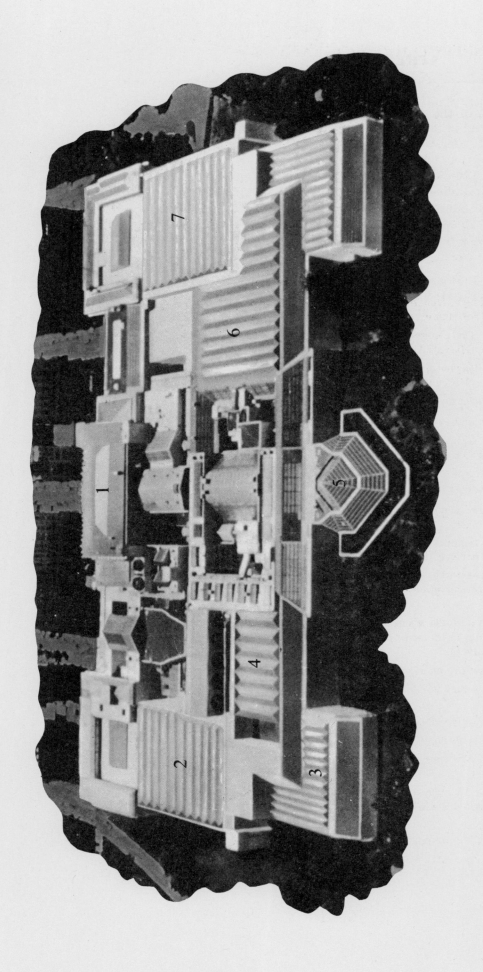

Bird's eye view of the Comprehensive Architectural Plan looking east with the edge of Central Park at bottom of photograph: 1 *Great Hall.* 2 *Sackler Wing.* *Temple of Dendur.* 3 *American Wing.* 4 *American Wing Garden Court and Park Entrance.* 5 *Lehman Pavilion.* 6 *European Wing Garden Court and Park Entrance (planned).* 7 *Michael C. Rockefeller Wing.*

SELECTED BIBLIOGRAPHY

BEAN, JACOB: *100 European Drawings in the Metropolitan Museum of Art*. (New York, 1964).

BEESON, NORA B., with SALINGER, MARGARETTA M.: *Guide to the Metropolitan Museum of Art*. (New York, 1972).

DAUTERMAN, CARL CHRISTIAN, and WATSON, F. J. B.: *The Wrightsman Collection: Volume III and IV, Furniture, Snuffboxes, Silver, Porcelain*. (New York, 1970).

ETTINGHAUSEN, RICHARD: *Islamic Art in the Metropolitan Museum of Art*. (New York, 1972).

FAHY, EVERETT, and WATSON, F. J. B.: *The Wrightsman Collection, Volume V, Paintings, Drawings, Sculpture*. (New York, 1973).

FREEMAN, MARGARET B.: *The Unicorn Tapestries*. (New York, 1976).

GRANCSAY, STEPHEN VINCENT: *Handbook of arms and armor, European and oriental, 4th edition with additions and corrections*. (New York, 1930).

HACKENBROCH, YVONNE: *The Untermyer Collection: Meissen and other Continental porcelain, faïence and enamel*. (Harvard University Press, 1956).

HAYES, WILLIAM C.: *The Scepter of Egypt: A Background for the Study of Egyptian Antiquities in the Metropolitan Museum of Art*. (New York, 1959).

HOWAT, JOHN K.: *The Hudson River and Its Painters*. (Viking Press, New York, 1972).

MAYOR, A. HYATT: *Prints and People: A Social History of Printed Pictures*. (New York, 1971).

MUSCARELLA, OSCAR WHITE: *Excavations at Agrab Tepe, Iran*. (New York, 1973).

MYERS, MARY L. *Architectural and Ornament Drawings: Juvarra, Vanvitelli, the Bibiena Family, and other Italian Draughtsmen*. (New York, 1975).

RICHTER, GISELA M. A.: *The Sculpture and Sculptors of the Greeks*. (New Haven, Conn., Yale University Press, 1970).

RORIMER, JAMES J. and KATHERINE SERRELL RORIMER: *Medieval monuments at The Cloisters: As they were and as They Are*. (New York, 1972).

STERLING, CHARLES, and SALINGER, MARGARETTA: *A Catalogue of French Paintings: XIX Century. Paintings in the Metropolitan by artists from Ingres to the Impressionists*. (New York, 1966).

STERLING, CHARLES, and SALINGER, MARGARETTA: *A Catalogue of French Paintings: XIX and XX Centuries. Paintings in the Metropolitan by Impressionists, Post-Impressionists, and Moderns*. (New York, 1966).

SZABO, GEORGE: *The Robert Lehman Collection*. (New York, 1975).

TRACY, BERRY B.: *19th-Century America: Furniture and other Decorative Arts*. (New York, 1970).

VALENSTEIN, SUZANNE G.: *A Handbook of Chinese Ceramics*. (New York, 1975).

VON BOTHMER, DIETRICH: *Attic black-figured amphorae*. (New York, 1963).

WILKINSON, CHARLES K.: *Nishapur: Pottery of the Early Islamic Period*. (New York, 1974).

WINTERNITZ, EMMANUEL: *Musical instruments of the Western world*. Photos by Lilly Stunzi. (New York, McGraw-Hill, 1967).

ZERI, FEDERICO and GARDNER, ELIZABETH E.: *A Catalogue of Italian Paintings: Florentine School* (131 paintings in the Metropolitan Museum). (New York, 1971).

ZERI, FEDERICO, and GARDNER, ELIZABETH E.: *A Catalogue of Italian Paintings: Venetian School* (110 paintings in the Metropolitan Museum). (New York, 1973).

INDEX OF ILLUSTRATIONS

Note: Italic Numbers refer to names mentioned in captions.

GENERAL INDEX